Alicia Whyle

Attract Who Want To Be

BOOK ONE

BASED ON A TRUE STORY

By: Alicia Hernandez-Whyle

Attract Who You Want To BE

Copyright © 2025 by Alicia Hernandez-Whyle

Published by: WP House

All rights reserved.

No part of this publication may be reproduced in any form or by any electronic or mechanical means, including information storage and retrieval systems, without written permission from the author, except for the use of brief quotations in a book review.

ISBN: 978-2-8529-3180-0

TABLE OF CONTENTS

INTRODUCTION 6

CHAPTER ONE: The Unexpected Journey Begins 8

CHAPTER TWO: The Weight of What's Coming 21

CHAPTER THREE: Attempting to Redefine My Future 30

CHAPTER FOUR: Building Resilience 45

CHAPTER FIVE: Educational Pursuits 58

CHAPTER SIX: Soaring Beyond Limits 73

CHAPTER SEVEN: The Pinnacle Moment 86

CHAPTER EIGHT: Rise Above The Ashes 92

CHAPTER NINE: Shifting Your Mindset for Success 106

CHAPTER TEN: Becoming Who You Want to Attract 117

CHAPTER ELEVEN: Lessons in the Rearview 134

CHAPTER TWELVE: Two Roads, One Choice 148

PART 1
FACING THE UNKNOWN

INTRODUCTION

This book is a deeply personal account of my journey through unimaginable pain, fierce determination, and ultimate victory. I'm sharing my story not just to open up about my struggles but to reach anyone who feels trapped in their own. Even in your darkest moments, your dreams are never out of reach.

But this book is about more than just hardship. It's about growth, strength, and discovering that success isn't just about accomplishments—it's about inner transformation. It's about rising from hopelessness and realizing that even when life doesn't go as planned, there is still purpose, still hope, and still a way forward.

As you walk through these pages with me, I hope you find encouragement and a reminder that no matter how broken or lost you feel, there is always a way out.

This is my story. May it inspire you to write your own.

CHAPTER ONE

The Unexpected Journey Begins

I vividly recall the moment when my pregnancy became known; to me, it was like a sudden slash in time. One second, life felt uncertain but normal. The next, everything changed. What started as just another anxious day quickly spiraled into one of the most defining moments of my life.

Attract Who You Want To BE

It was a routine visit to the doctor, a follow-up to the persistent health issues that had troubled me. My mother, with a concerned expression marked on her face, accompanied me to the clinic, a subtle hint of her increasing worry. After a thorough examination and a series of tests, the diagnosis came in; I was two months pregnant—yeah, you heard that right, two months preggo.

The doctor's words, though spoken in clinical tones, were anything but impersonal to me. "You're pregnant," he said, his voice steady but the gravity of the news unmistakable. Those two words—"you're pregnant"—were more than just a statement of fact; they were a major shake-up in my reality. It was demeaning and felt like a bad dream—like what I was hearing wasn't real. My heart pounded fiercely in my chest. A sudden wave of fear took over me, leaving me unable to fully grasp what was happening. I was terrified of what was going to happen to me, not to mention the thought of having to see the doctor share the news with my mom.

As the doctor shared the diagnosis with my mom, her tone cut through the air, heavy with disappointment. The shock and disapproval in her eyes seemed to magnify the turmoil I felt within. A chill crept through my body, the weight of the situation pressing on me in a way that left me momentarily frozen.

The most devastating part was knowing I had fallen short of my mom's expectations. As a single mother raising five children, I had witnessed the endless sacrifices she made and the tireless effort she poured into our lives. My greatest wish had always been to make her proud, and now, the thought of failing her felt like a crushing burden within my soul.

Her reaction during the car ride home was more profound than words could express. The heavy silence between us was like an invisible wall, thick with unspoken emotions. Each mile felt endless, the air filled with a quiet tension that seemed to drive a wedge between us.

Once home, the conversations about what to do next were painfully raw. My mom firmly believed that an abortion was the only way to salvage my future. Her unyielding and resolute voice gave me the impression that someone else had already decided my choices for me. The arguments that followed were deeply emotional, each word charged with the frustration and fear that had taken over our home. My mother's focus was solely on erasing the pregnancy and pushing me back toward school. She was desperate to protect me from the shame she feared would follow me, or maybe her, as my belly grew.

A few hours later, I found myself breaking down completely, tears streaming down my face as I buried it in my pillow. I held the pillow tightly, the fabric damp with my sobs, and let myself cry through the night. The reality of the doctor's voice still echoed in my mind, each word stabbing through me with the harsh truth: I was pregnant.

The news of my pregnancy also stirred up a deep sense of shame within me. Growing up, I had always strived to meet the expectations placed upon me as a Christian to make choices that would align with God's word. I felt as though I had let everyone down, not only myself but also my Sunday school teacher and my mother, whose vision for my future seemed to unravel before her. Her disappointed gaze reflected the shame I felt inside, each look and comment cutting through my already fragile sense of self-worth.

Fear gripped me with a suffocating intensity. What did this mean for my future? What would the world think of me? How would I handle the responsibilities of motherhood? Not to mention the poverty that weighed heavily on my family during that time only added to the burden I was already facing.

In the days that followed, the stark reality of my pregnancy eclipsed any sense of joy or excitement that others might associate with such news. The thought of facing my family's reaction, enduring their disappointment, and addressing the countless challenges of both the immediate and distant future left me feeling completely overwhelmed.

Alicia Whyle

When Truth Hits Home

When my siblings heard the news, their reactions were a mixture of shock, disbelief, and concern. Initially, my elder sibling, who typically assumed a protective role, expressed anger, which stemmed from a deep fear for my future. They worried about how I would manage such a monumental responsibility at such a young age. As we talked, their frustration softened into a cautious acceptance, though their words carried a warning: "This isn't going to be easy."

My younger sister, on the other hand, was visibly confused. Too young to fully grasp the weight of the situation, she simply asked, "Are you going to be okay?" Their innocent question brought tears to my eyes, reminding me of the ripple effect my choices had on those around me.

Not everyone showed concern for my well-being, though. My aunt and grandmother, who had never shown me affection or support even before my pregnancy, became even more distant and cold. There were countless nights filled with arguments between my aunts, my mother, and me. My aunt was pushing for an abortion like it was her decision to make.

Meanwhile, my boyfriend's reaction added another layer of complexity to my emotional turmoil. Initially, his excitement about becoming a father seemed like a glimmer of hope in my darkened world. At first he was excited, but as the weeks passed by, all excitement left. He began coming around less frequently, showing up only once a week and staying for only brief visits. It was as though he had shifted his focus from me and my pregnancy to hanging out with his friends.

His abandonment left me heartbroken and completely alone. Each visit that fell short of what I needed only deepened the pain, leaving me trapped in sleepless nights with my tears as my only companion. A deep sense of isolation and hopelessness consumed me daily.

His family's cruel judgments and nasty rumors about my baby's paternity amplified my already low self-esteem. Their disrespect felt like a salve on an already raw wound.

Facing the Hopeless Future

The following weeks were a whirlwind of arguments and heartache. My mother's insistence on abortion clashed with my determination to keep the baby. Her fears of shame and societal judgment weighed heavily on her decisions, but I couldn't let go of the life growing within me.

Weeks after finding out I was pregnant, I received a call from the doctor, asking about my last menstrual cycle. The question felt off, making me uneasy. I didn't understand what was happening, so I went straight to my mom. When I told her about the call, she said, without hesitation, that the doctor was going to perform an abortion on me.

Shock hit me like a wave. My heart pounded as I stared at her, disbelief turning into anger. "Why do I need an abortion? What are you trying to do to me?" I shouted, my voice shaking with fear. "What if I can never have another baby?"

My mom, clearly frustrated, snapped back, "You're worried about having a baby instead of focusing on your education!" We argued for what felt like hours, both of us hurt and lashing out, not truly hearing each other.

The idea of ending the pregnancy was impossible for me to accept. I couldn't bring myself to extinguish a life that had no say in my bad decisions.

After arguing back and forth, my mom said, "Fine. Keep it if you want," she said, her voice devoid of warmth. "But don't expect me to raise this child." This is your problem, not mine, she said. She then left for work, leaving me alone with my emotions. Even though I get to keep my baby, the tension was thick between Mom and me, the pain between us almost unbearable. We were both hurting so much; only God could have healed the wounds we both carried that day.

Breaking Under the Burden

Within the next month, things went from difficult to unbearable. The morning sickness was relentless, and it wasn't just in the mornings—it came at all hours, every single day, wearing me down. It felt like it was slowly eating away at my already slim frame, and with each passing day, I grew weaker. The nausea was constant, leaving me unable to keep anything down, and the exhaustion was devastating. My body ached in ways I never imagined possible, and I felt like I was trapped in a cycle of pain with no way out.

I couldn't bear it. The pain and sickness consumed me, and there were moments when I thought I couldn't face another day. Each wave of nausea felt like it was stripping away not just my physical strength, but my willpower, too. My life felt utterly hopeless, like I was drowning in a sea of misery with no lifeline in sight. I kept wondering, "When will this be over?" How much longer can I endure this?

To make matters worse, there was no one to comfort me or give a word of encouragement. I experienced a profound sense of isolation, as though the entire world had abandoned me. My aunts and other relatives had pushed me away, their silence and indifference crushing what little hope I had left. I longed for someone to understand, to hold my hand and tell me I wasn't alone, but no one did. There was no love, warmth, or comforting words that came from anyone.

I had never felt so lost—so abandoned. I found myself ensnared in this intolerable reality, facing sickness, fear, and loneliness alone. My life felt loveless, and in those moments of despair, I couldn't see any way out. I yearn for the pain to stop, for everything to be over with.

There was no planning for the future. I had no money, and neither did the father of the baby. I could only take things one day at a time, trying to handle each moment as best as I could.

Every day was a struggle, and I yearned for some relief, some sense of normalcy. All I wanted was for the baby to be out of me—to escape the constant discomfort and immense pressure. It felt like I was trapped in an endless cycle of worry and pain, with nothing but the hope that someday things would get better for me.

Somehow, I held onto that hope, believing that eventually my life would return to some semblance of normal. But that day never came. With no education, no job, and a baby on the way, I found myself sharing a room with my siblings, feeling stupid and helpless.

I hated being pregnant, especially since I had no friends and felt disconnected from any kind of life I once knew. The dreams of relief and normalcy seemed to drift further away, replaced by the reality of ongoing hardship and a profound sense of loneliness.

Branded by Judgment

During my pregnancy as a teen mom, the pressure of society's expectations and the judgment from others seemed just as heavy as the personal challenges I faced. From the moment my pregnancy became known, I sensed the relentless, unforgiving gaze of society. I felt a deep sense of betrayal, as if I had been left to face judgment alone, with no support in sight.

People no longer viewed me as a hopeful, bright, and ambitious teenager, but rather as a cautionary tale—a statistic to avoid.

Alicia Whyle

In my community, teenage pregnancy is scrutinized through a harsh and narrow lens. The prevailing expectation is that teenagers should focus on education and personal development, and any deviation from this norm is met with scorn. My pregnancy wasn't just a personal issue; it became a public spectacle, subject to intense judgment and criticism.

At sixteen, I was expected to be a model student working toward a promising future. Instead, I found myself in a situation that seemed to contradict these expectations. The societal pressure to conform made me feel like a profound failure.

The constant whispers and harsh judgments drenched me in a sea of shame and disappointment. Words such as "irresponsible" and "whore" circulated, intensifying my feeling of isolation. I was completely shut out from social circles. I became an unwelcome presence in spaces where I once felt safe. Due to this, I stayed inside almost every day. My social life disappeared. Not only had I become a social outcast, but I also had no friends and no longer attended school.

Every glance from the community felt like a piercing reminder of my situation. I even faced disdain from a particular woman and her daughters, who would look at me and speak ill of me as I passed by, adding to my sense of despair.

Coping with Judgement

Enduring the weight of judgment was an agonizing experience. Every glance from the community felt like a silent condemnation, a piercing reminder of the situation I found myself in.

The humiliation was unbearable, and I found myself turning to prayer, begging God to hide my growing belly from the world. Miraculously, my prayer seemed answered in a way I hadn't anticipated—my belly remained relatively small throughout most of my pregnancy. It wasn't until I was eight months along that people began to see my belly. They knew I was pregnant, but it was not visible for them to see. Somehow, not having a noticeably big belly gave me a sense of peace when I ventured outside my community.

God's mercy provided me with a brief respite from the relentless judgment that had been hanging over me.

Still, avoidance became my primary means of coping. I altered my daily routine, taking longer routes to sidestep encounters with those who might sneer or whisper behind my back. At times, I confined myself indoors for weeks, retreating from the world in an attempt to escape the scrutiny that followed me like a shadow.

Although these actions shielded me from immediate criticism, they only made me feel more isolated, leaving scars that stayed long after the whispers faded.

Looking back, I see how much their condemnation shaped my thoughts and emotions. Their words, their silence, their disgust—each one reinforced the belief that I was unworthy. I began to internalize their judgment, convincing myself that I was a failure, someone the world had no place for. And so, I hid—not just my body, but the person I was becoming.

Chapter one only provided a glimpse of the impending storm. As I stepped into the unknown, Chapter Two would unleash the raw intensity of what was to come—the overwhelming force of change, the weight of everything that would soon collide, and the delivery that would forever alter my world.

CHAPTER TWO

The Weight of What's Coming

Life has a way of shifting in an instant, leaving you staring into a reality you never saw coming. When I first found out I was pregnant, it felt as though the ground beneath me cracked open, pulling me into a nightmare I couldn't escape. This isn't happening to me, I kept telling myself. Maybe the test was wrong, or if I just ignored it long enough, it would disappear. I clung to these lies, hoping that if I pretended hard enough, the morning sickness and everything else would just fade away. But denial can only shield you for so long, and the truth was waiting to break through.

From Denial to Acceptance

Denial was my refuge, a way to avoid the reality that was slowly creeping in. But denial only lasts so long. Soon, the little things I tried to ignore started adding up. My clothes didn't fit right, and my stomach began to grow. Each day felt heavier than the last, as the reality of what was happening grew impossible to ignore. The weight of it, knowing my life was about to change forever, pressed down on me. I could no longer flee or conceal it. My body was betraying me, showing me daily what I wasn't ready to accept.

Every time I looked in the mirror, I saw a stranger staring back at me—someone who was no longer just a carefree teenager but someone trapped by a decision I couldn't undo. My heart ached with disappointment. I had dreams. I had plans. Instead of facing the consequences of my careless choices, I should have been preparing for my graduation.

Attract Who You Want To BE

I really couldn't stop thinking of how I had ruined everything. Deeply rooted in my conscience, the guilt was difficult to break free from. I was angry at myself for being so reckless, for not thinking things through, for letting my life spiral out of control.

And then there was the shame. The quiet, nagging shame was a constant presence in my mind. I had always been one with potential, someone who was going to do great things. But now? Now, all I saw was the end of those dreams. I wasn't ready for this. I wasn't ready to be responsible for another life when I could barely handle my own.

It was not only about losing my old self but also about embracing a new version of myself that I didn't recognize. My pregnancy cut me off, leaving me feeling alone and terrified about the future. Trapped in this new reality with no clear way forward, the weight of uncertainty crushed me. Every night, I cried myself to sleep, wishing for some way to undo it all, to go back to being that carefree girl who hadn't yet made a decision that would change her life forever.

Everything was happening so quickly, and there was no turning back. After choosing to keep the baby, I had to accept my pregnancy, whether I was ready or not. That baby would be arriving in just a few months, and I knew I had to find a way to face the situation head-on, to cope with the racing emotions, and to prepare myself for the immense responsibility that lay ahead.

Taking care of my health now had to become a priority, not just for me but for my baby. That meant eating foods I disliked and forcing myself to take tablets I hated. Simple things I once took for granted—lifting heavy objects, running, jumping, and enjoying life without restrictions—were now out of reach. Accepting this new reality was not a choice but a necessity, becoming more evident with each passing week.

Months after finding out I was pregnant, I finally joined a clinic for prenatal care. The experience was far from pleasant. The nurses bombarded me with questions that seemed to magnify my shame and insecurities. Every inquiry felt like an invasion, making me feel even more exposed and vulnerable.

Despite my efforts to appear older and somehow match the seriousness of my situation, my youthful appearance made it clear that I was still very young. The milk-like softness of my face only accentuated my teenage years, often leading people to guess my age as fourteen. Seeing myself so young and pregnant was disheartening and humiliating.

Yet in the midst of everything, I found myself turning to the only place I could seek solace—prayer. I poured out my heart to God when the weight of my reality felt like it was crushing me, and I couldn't talk to anyone about what I was going through. Each word felt like a desperate plea, as if my entire world relied on those moments of connection. I asked for forgiveness for my stupid choices, for the innocence I had lost. The tears often flowed freely as I cried out for reassurance, feeling so unworthy yet longing for peace.

I felt so unprepared to face what was coming. Yet, in those quiet reflections, through the comforting words of scripture, I found a glimmer of strength. I didn't have all the answers, and fear still clawed at me, but maybe, just maybe, I could find my way through this with God by my side. Despite the staggering pain of my situation, I realize that I wasn't completely a lost cause during those moments.

Alone in the Waiting Room

As I continued to attend my prenatal appointments, each visit was a wave of anxiety crashing over me. I attended the clinic alone, feeling vulnerable and anxious with all eyes on me. Facing new doctors and nurses felt like an ordeal, as I had to constantly explain my situation and relive the shame each time.

The emotional weight of carrying a child on my own felt heavy, and the lack of a solid support network made every challenge feel even more intense—a burden I had to carry alone. No one I know was there to listen to my worries or talk about my emotions. I felt completely empty, as if happiness had vanished from my life. Although my mom didn't kick me out and continued to provide for my basic needs, I longed for more love and understanding from her.

Occasionally, a small comfort would come when my baby moved—a flutter that reminded me he was okay—but even that fleeting joy was shadowed by my intense sadness.

Unprepared for Motherhood

Returning to school during and after my pregnancy felt like an impossible dream. The thought of walking those familiar hallways, knowing I would face the whispers and stares, made my stomach churn with dread. The embarrassment of my bad choices, visible to everyone, was too much for me to endure.

Without a job of my own, I was now dependent on my baby's father, who worked a grueling nine-to-five for barely above minimum wage. The thought of relying on others felt like a heavy burden, stripping me of my sense of independence.

I could feel his frustration as well. We were both so young, caught in a situation we both weren't prepared for, trying to figure out how to handle a situation that felt way too big for us. Without a plan in place, we felt like lost teenagers, desperately trying to do what was right for our baby.

My chest tightened with anxiety as I considered all the expenses—diapers, baby gear, and healthcare. The desire to create a stable environment for my child became a fierce urgency, but the harsh reality of our financial struggles loomed like a dark cloud, casting a shadow over any hopes I dared to entertain.

There was no space for a nursery, no beautifully arranged baby room like the ones I had seen in magazines. All I had was a secondhand crib, a gift from someone who took pity on my situation. I did my best to make it look presentable, dressing it up with soft blankets and a few small decorations. But no matter how much I tried, it was still just a crib in the corner of a room I shared with my siblings—a quiet reminder of how unprepared I was for the life ahead. As much as I wanted to do more for my baby's arrival, I couldn't.

Alicia Whyle

The Pain and Triumph of Delivery

After nine long months of carrying my son, the moment had finally come for him to enter the world. The delivery was an agonizing experience, one filled with pain and stress, made worse by the rude comments and harsh treatment from the nurses. They treated me like I was less than human. Their lack of empathy deeply affected me, leaving me feeling utterly scared and helpless—just a scared teenager in a hospital gown. Every contraction felt like a powerful force, each one pushing me to my limits.

In that delivery room, all I could focus on was getting over this pain and having my baby here safely. I thought about my boyfriend and my mother waiting anxiously in the waiting room, their faces etched with concern. I knew I had disappointed my mom by getting pregnant so young, and though I didn't have her gentle love throughout my pregnancy, she was still there, supporting me through one of the toughest moments of my life.

Finally, after what felt like an eternity, my baby was born. I remember him clearly—fair skin, with soft, curly hair, weighing in at seven pounds. When the nurse laid him on my chest, a rush of love and protectiveness surged through me. It was the first time in months that I felt a sense of joy and happiness. I kissed his little head and whispered, "I promise not to let anything bad ever happen to you." At just seventeen, I had become a mother, a title I wore with a heavy heart.

After a few days, the hospital finally released my baby and me. My baby grandmother by his dad's side came to visit, bringing diapers and baby clothes, her eyes lighting up as she held him. She looked down at his little face and instantly recognized her grandson's features. It was a moment of undeniable affirmation—the child's paternity was clear, and that realization brought a sense of peace. Watching her cradle him, I felt a wave of joy rush through me. It wasn't much, but it was the acceptance I had longed for, even if it didn't extend to me. As long as they saw him as their grandson, that was the assurance I needed.

With the birth of my son, the weight of my new reality settled in, but despite the numerous challenges, I was determined to redefine my future. Little did I know that the journey to change my situation would be filled with trial after trial, each attempt leaving me more uncertain than the last.

CHAPTER THREE

Attempting to Redefine My Future

At seventeen, I found myself holding a baby boy in my arms—a little life that depended entirely on me, even though I knew almost nothing about being a mother. Nothing could have prepared me for the immense responsibility of motherhood.

Day after day, I was bombarded by endless cries that pierced through the quiet nights, cries I was desperate to soothe but often didn't know how. The nights felt endless, each one spent rocking and pacing, trying to calm the tiny cries that seemed to mirror the fears and doubts within me.

I could only dream of the comfort of sleep; exhaustion weighed me down, leaving me completely drained. Some nights, as I rocked him to sleep, tears would quietly fall. How would I ever rebuild the life I once knew?

My body felt exhausted, and my emotions were in disarray. Looking in the mirror, I barely recognized the person staring back—a reflection of someone weighed down by everything happening around me.

The changes in my body only added to my daily stress. My once-flat belly was now a canvas of stretched and marked skin, a reminder of how much my life had shifted. My chest, something I'd rarely thought about before, had become a source of nourishment for my son. Each feeding left me feeling worn out. I hated the image staring back at me in the mirror. I hadn't had the chance to embrace or enjoy my body before it transformed. Now, every glance brought a wave of regret and frustration, mourning a version of myself I'd never taken the time to appreciate.

My self-esteem plummeted, and I couldn't shake the feeling that I had lost something I couldn't get back. I was just a teenager—yet here I was, a mother, exhausted, afraid, and silently mourning the person I once was.

At times, I felt jealous of my friends as I observed them living their lives; witnessing their joy and independence from a distance served as a constant reminder of everything I had lost. It hurt deeply, knowing that while they could go out and make memories, my days were now defined by responsibilities I hadn't been ready to shoulder.

I longed for just a few moments of escape, a fleeting chance to feel like myself again. Carefree moments I once took for granted were now replaced by an endless cycle of diapers and feedings.

After enduring heartbreak and longing to be someone else, I eventually accepted that those lost moments were gone forever. My life was no longer my own—it now revolved around my son and the immense responsibility of raising him. I resolved to let go of longing for friendship and the freedom I once had. Instead, I convinced myself that my purpose was rooted in being a mother, dedicating all my energy to giving my son the love and care he deserved.

But as much as I tried to convince myself that motherhood was my sole purpose, a nagging thought remained—I couldn't let my life stall here. I had a choice to make.

I was at a crossroads, faced with two choices. I could either keep feeling sorry for myself and let everything weigh me down, or I could start taking action and try to build a better life for my son and me. I knew it was time to stop moping and start making decisions that actually mattered. This was my life now, my responsibility, and it was up to me to make something out of it.

I was determined to make every moment count, to transform my struggles into strength for both of us.

Fighting for a Better Tomorrow

When my son reached eight months, something clicked within me. I realized I couldn't keep putting off the changes I needed to make. I knew I needed to find a job, one that would help us live more comfortably. Every day, I actively searched for job opportunities, submitting numerous applications in the hopes of starting something new. However, it wasn't as easy as I thought it would be. My applications were rejected by numerous employers. Each rejection shattered my confidence.

Without my CXC certificate from high school, it felt like every door was slamming shut in my face. Since I hadn't finished high school, each 'no' made the weight of my situation feel even heavier. I was now asking myself over and over how things were so hard for me. I wanted to blame someone, anyone—but deep down, I knew there was no one to blame but myself. I had made choices, and now I had to face the consequences. Despite everything, I couldn't afford to quit. My son's little face was a constant reminder of the responsibility I carried. His eyes, full of trust, pushed me to keep going, even when every part of me felt exhausted.

As the weeks dragged on, the rejections piled up, and so did the frustration. I had always thought that if you tried hard enough, someone would notice and care. But no one did. It was as if society had decided I wasn't worth the chance, and that realization broke something inside me.

Still, I kept pushing. I couldn't bear the thought of my son growing up to feel the same sense of hopelessness that I did. He was my reason to fight, even when it felt like I had nothing left to give.

Attract Who You Want To BE

During these challenging times, the significance of education became evident. My parents had always drilled into me the importance of schooling, insisting that it was the gateway to a better future. Yet, it took the harsh reality of my situation to finally grasp their wisdom.

All those job rejections fueled a growing sense of urgency within me to reclaim my education. I believed that if I could get my CXC passes, my self-esteem would rise, and I'd finally be in a position to secure a well-paying job that would allow me to give my son the life I knew he deserved—something I couldn't provide at that moment.

With a fire ignited within me, I composed a heartfelt letter to the Ministry of Education, pouring out my soul in the hopes that the desperation behind my words would be seen. I laid bare my story as a teenage mother, pleading for a second chance in the school system. I hoped that it would have resonated with the minister. As the weeks went by with no response, the weight of not knowing what would happen next started to grow heavier.

Then, one day, I received a letter—the Minister of Education wanted to meet with me. I read the words over and over, a mix of disbelief and excitement flooding through me. It felt surreal, like something I had only hoped for but never actually expected. This could be the break I had been waiting for.

Alicia Whyle

On the day of the interview, I dressed in my best office attire, determined to convey my seriousness and professionalism. As I stepped into the minister's office, my nerves threatened to overpower me, but I pushed them aside. I shook his hand, took a seat, and poured out my story, hoping for understanding and compassion.

The meeting I had waited weeks for lasted only ten minutes, and then he told me I was too old to return to the school system. With desperation in my voice, I said, "Please, I'm only seventeen." I told him there are students older than me still in secondary school. I pleaded my case, desperate to make him see how committed I was to my education now that I was a mother. I expressed my desire for my son to overcome the poverty I had experienced, but my pleas met with silence.

As I walked out of his office crying, a deep sense of disappointment settled in. All my efforts felt wasted, and failure wrapped around me like a shroud. Every sense of motivation I had in me left my body at that moment. What was I going to do now? The thought of private school was laughable since I had no job and no savings.

My mother's disappointment in me had clouded her judgment, leading her to stay home instead of attending the meeting with me. Had she shown her support, perhaps the minister would have recognized my determination and given me the chance to reclaim my education.

Unfortunately, I took my education for granted, and losing the chance to graduate is a haunting memory I carried with me every single day.

My heart longs for a do-over, for a chance to rewrite my story. The regret I carry is a heavy burden, and I often find myself wondering how different my life could have been if I had only valued my education as I should have. I can't help but reflect on the moments where I veered off course, each one contributing to the path I find myself on now.

Wasted Opportunity

At the age of eighteen, I was presented with an unexpected opportunity. The government introduced a six-month program that offered the chance to learn a new skill, along with a stipend each month. While the stipend wasn't much, I saw it as a valuable stepping stone—an opportunity that can add some value to my resume. It will also make caring for my son's needs much easier, giving me a sense of independence and relief, knowing I didn't have to rely on anyone else, even if only for a short while. This opportunity was more than just a program—it was a chance to reshape my future with a fresh start.

This new chapter brought with it unexpected support. My mother stood firmly behind my decision, offering her support by babysitting my son while I attended the program each day. Her sacrifice filled me with gratitude, as it felt like she was starting to believe in what I could do. Each morning, I donned the program's special uniform, which took me back to the structure of school. I was filled with anticipation as I stepped into a new routine, eager to learn about geriatric nursing and life skills that would enhance my daily life. As my routine settled in, so did the sense of belonging in a new environment—one that, for the first time in a long while, gave me a taste of the freedom I had missed.

It was such a relief to escape the confines of my home and finally be able to be around other my age. I was ready to learn something new, and I reveled in the fun and new friendships that came with it. As I made friends and became a part of this new journey, I felt a sense of excitement. However, underlying my excitement was a burden of secrecy. I chose to keep my son a secret from my new friends, haunted by the fear that if they discovered I was a teenage mother, they might judge me harshly like my previous friends had. Despite the joy of forming new friendships, a part of me was still tethered to the past, haunted by fears of judgment.

Attract Who You Want To BE

It hurt to keep such an important part of my life hidden, as it seemed like I was ashamed of my son. But the weight of being a teenage mother lingered heavily, and the embarrassment was hard to shake off. I wanted to embrace this new chapter, to be proud of who I had become, yet the shadow of my past was always there, reminding me of the hurdles I still had to face.

These new friends filled a void that had lingered in my life since I became a teenage mom. For so long, I felt isolated, cut off from the carefree moments of youth. But now, surrounded by their laughter and energy, I experienced a sense of joy I had almost forgotten existed.

I wore a mask daily when I was around my new friends, pretending that I wasn't a mother, lying to myself in the process. But in those moments of laughter and excitement, I was momentarily elated. However, in my excitement, I overlooked how easily I was slipping back into my old lifestyle—the same one that had led me to become pregnant at sixteen.

Every weekend, the calls poured in, inviting me to join in their adventures. I found myself pleading with my sister to babysit, desperate for a chance to reclaim the fun I had lost while pregnant with my first son.

Alicia Whyle

Partying became my escape, my way of grasping at the remnants of youth I feared I had lost forever. Yet, with every night out, I buried my darkest secret deeper, praying that no one would uncover the truth I desperately tried to hide.

With each moment spent away from my responsibilities, I felt my connection to my son drifting further away—a constant reminder that I wasn't free like them. I was a mother, grappling with the loss of a life I once loved.

I had walked into the institute filled with plans and dreams, convinced that this time would be different. I had the motivation, but I was still weighed down by a mindset of mediocrity. My focus slipped from the start, drawn away by old habits and the irresistible pull of fleeting distractions I couldn't seem to break free from.

Despite my best intentions, I struggled to stay on course. Geriatric nursing was my chosen path, a course I believed would lead to a better future. Yet, every time I tried to buckle down, the longing to reclaim my carefree teenage years always managed to pull me away.

When graduation day arrived, I wasn't standing with pride or a sense of accomplishment. Instead, I stood there, grappling with the weight of regret. I realized that my lack of focus had caught up with me. In my hands wasn't a certificate in geriatric nursing, the proof of my hard work and dedication—instead it was a participation award.

It served as a hollow reminder of how I had allowed distractions to derail me, leaving my dreams unfulfilled. I hadn't accomplished my mission to build a brighter future for me and my son. Instead, I found myself back at the beginning, lacking the education necessary to unlock new possibilities.

In that moment, I realized that something had to change—not just my actions, but my mindset. If I didn't shift my thinking, I might as well say goodbye to any chance at a bright future.

Despite the weight of disappointment pressing on me, I found myself feeling a quiet, unexpected gratitude for the opportunity I'd been given—a chance I now recognized had greatly opened my eyes to see that I needed to work on myself. It helped me realize that if the Ministry of Education had given me the chance to return to school full-time, I most likely would have wasted it like I did with this program. The pull toward having fun with friends and misplaced priorities would have taken over because the desire to relive the life I once had was still too strong within me. I was longing for the youthful days of my adolescence—a time filled with companionship, excitement, and independence, free from the weight of being a young mother.

Alicia Whyle

While my journey had been marked by missed opportunities, I had gained clarity about the person I wanted to become and the life I wanted to build for my son. Little did I know, the next chapter of my life would test me in ways I never imagined.

Attract Who You Want To BE

Alicia Whyle

PART 2

THE REFINING FIRE

CHAPTER FOUR

Building Resilience

There comes a moment when doubt creeps in louder than ambition. Every effort feels like a misstep, and the path ahead is anything but clear. As time went by, the burden of failure felt suffocating; each rejection made me wonder if I'd ever find a way forward. I lacked a job, the necessary qualifications, and a clear direction, leaving me uncertain if my efforts even mattered. Every door I knocked on stayed shut, and every attempt seemed to crumble before my eyes. However, as I persistently sought ways to enhance my life by applying for jobs and pursuing opportunities, I refused to give up. I felt a quiet determination rising within me, a spark of hope refusing to be extinguished.

The Power of Taking Chances

One sunny morning, while I was waiting by the hospital building, a stranger struck up a conversation with me about a job vacancy at a call center. She told me to apply, and she mentioned the qualifications I'd need. I listened, even though deep down, I knew I didn't meet the requirements.

Still, I projected confidence, always acting as though I was highly qualified, no matter where I went. It was my way of hiding the embarrassment of having to explain my past or admit that I was a high school dropout. The thought of revealing that part of my journey felt like a vulnerability I couldn't afford to expose.

Hearing about the job made me reflect on just how much I lacked the qualifications employers were looking for. No matter how confidently I carried myself, I couldn't escape the reality that I didn't have a CXC certificate. More than once, I entertained the idea of fraudulently obtaining a CXC certificate, as it seemed like a convenient solution, a shortcut to the future I longed for. However, I deeply understood that choosing the easy path would never lead to genuine success.

Even though I didn't have the CXC passes she said were necessary, something within me—what I now recognize as the Holy Spirit—urged me to go ahead and apply anyway. A quiet yet powerful prompting pushed me to take a risk, despite the challenges.

That morning, despite the long and exhausting journey, I made my way to the call center—miles away from home. The distance didn't matter. I was willing to sacrifice comfort for the possibility of a breakthrough. With unwavering faith, I walked into the building and boldly submitted my application, choosing to believe that, despite the odds, this could be my chance.

A few weeks later, my phone rang. The moment I had been waiting for had finally arrived—an invitation for an interview. My heart leaped with excitement; was this really my chance? Would they see past my lack of qualifications and give me a chance? Doubt lingered, but so did hope.

On the day of the interview, my heart raced with nerves as I sat in the waiting room, trying to calm myself. I prayed silently and earnestly, pleading with God to grant me this opportunity. I needed this—for myself, but most importantly, for my son.

When the interviewer finally called my name, I felt both dread and determination as I stepped into the room. The HR manager smiled politely and began asking questions. Then came the one I was dreading: "Do you have your CXC certificate with you?" I told her I didn't have any since I did not finish school. Her smile faltered, and for a moment, I thought the interview was over.

But then, to my surprise, she handed me a test and said, "We require five CXC passes, but let's see how you do on this math test." My nerves were on edge as I stared at the paper, but I pushed through, knowing this might be my only chance. Question by question, I fought back self-doubt and focused as hard as I could.

When I handed back the completed test, I felt a mixture of relief and uncertainty. A few moments later, the manager looked up from the paper with a raised eyebrow. "You passed," she said, almost as if she hadn't expected it.

For a moment, I felt a glimmer of excitement, but it was quickly deflated when she mentioned again that the position required five CXC passes.

My stomach knotted as I admitted, once more, that I didn't have any. I braced myself for rejection, but the look on her face shifted. There was no dismissal, no outright refusal. Instead, she seemed to be weighing something in her mind.

What happened next took me by complete surprise. Instead of turning me away, she said, "I'm going to give you this job." Then, she gave me a heartfelt lecture about the importance of education and encouraged me to return to school. In that moment, I was forever grateful that I met that interviewer that day. It was as if God had softened her heart, helping her see past my shortcomings and giving me a chance—a chance I had been longing for ever since I had my son.

Overcome with emotion, I found it hard to comprehend the magnitude of her kindness. I felt a rush of gratitude wash over me, realizing that my prayers were being answered. I had been looking for jobs in grocery stores, restaurants, and similar places, never imagining I'd end up working in a call center, sitting in an office cubicle in one of the most prestigious buildings in my country.

Within my heart, I had always believed that God had a plan for my life, and in that moment, I felt that plan was finally starting to unfold. It reminded us that sometimes moving forward depends on our faith and boldness rather than our qualifications.

Looking back, I realized that this mindset—choosing to carry myself as if I already had what I needed to land the job—played a crucial role in landing this job. Because I moved with boldness and took action despite my doubts, I was able to attract an opportunity I didn't technically qualify for. It felt as though faith unlocked opportunities for me, even when logic suggested they should remain closed.

Now, with this job in hand, I had more than just a paycheck; it was a stepping stone to a brighter future, and I was ready to embrace the possibilities that lay ahead. With a stable income, I could finally start saving and take steps toward going back to school.

The Turnaround

Everything began to change when my son's father landed a well-paying job at a restaurant. With both of us earning an income, the heavy burdens on my shoulders began to lessen. He started showering me with gifts and affection, each gesture a clear attempt to make up for everything that had gone wrong during our relationship. But as I accepted each token, doubt crept in. Was this real, or was it just another fleeting moment of kindness that would disappear as quickly as it had arrived? I couldn't shake the feeling that this new tenderness might be temporary, just a brief break before the storm returned. Yet, even as uncertainty lingered in my heart, there was one thing I couldn't deny—our son's joy whenever his father walked through the door.

The moment the door creaked open, my son's eyes sparkled with excitement. He dropped his toy, sprinted toward his father, and flung his tiny arms around his legs, giggling as if the world had just gifted him his greatest joy. His father took pride in ensuring that he had everything he needed, and I couldn't help but feel proud for the way he stepped up. God was truly providing for us, and I felt blessed to witness the bond between them grow stronger every day.

As if that wasn't enough, his dad started taking our son to visit his mother, giving me precious time to myself that I desperately needed. Those quiet moments gave me a much-needed break, helping me recharge for work the next day.

This job changed everything for me. Gone were the feelings of stress and worthlessness that had weighed me down for so long. Instead, I began to feel a newfound sense of confidence and pride, knowing that I was finally doing something positive with my life. With this newfound sense of purpose, I approached my job with renewed energy. It wasn't long before my hard work paid off in a way I never expected.

Alicia Whyle

After working at the call center for a few months, I was shocked when my name was called for an award recognizing 100% customer satisfaction. I was not expecting it—after all, I had dealt with some of the most difficult and abusive customers. Yet, no matter how harsh the calls got, I had always chosen to remain calm and respectful. Holding that award made me feel a sense of accomplishment. It was proof that I was more than my past, that I was capable and valuable.

Just when I thought things couldn't get any better, a surprising opportunity followed the recognition for my excellent customer service.

Nine months into the job, my supervisor called me in for a meeting. My heart pounded as I sat across from her, wondering what this was about. Then she said the words that left me completely stunned—she was offering me a promotion to a supervisory role. I blinked, struggling to process it. Me? A supervisor? I was thrilled, but at the same time, I was feeling a bit cautious. My resume clearly stated I had no CXC passes, so she had to know I wasn't technically qualified for the job. And yet, she had chosen me. At that moment, I knew—this was nothing short of God's favor.

I was overjoyed about this promotion—it meant more financial stability and a real opportunity for my child's father and me to build a better life. Maybe now, we could finally afford to rent an apartment and start living together as a family. When I got pregnant at sixteen, my mom refused to let me move in with him, and at the time, I had no choice but to accept it. But now, at twenty, things had changed. I was an adult, ready to take control of my future and create a home for us—a space where we could truly be a family.

From Breakthrough to Breakdown

As my son grew, I marveled at his fearless curiosity, his bright laughter weaving its way into the hearts of everyone he encountered. His intelligence and well-behaved nature drew people in, and I couldn't help but beam with pride. He was a radiant light, shining brightly in every room.

As my son thrived and life seemed to be improving, a sudden twist of fate turned everything upside down, shattering the sense of stability I had worked so hard to build.

I had barely settled into my new role as a supervisor, still riding the wave of excitement from my promotion, when I found out I was pregnant again.

Alicia Whyle

The news profoundly affected me, leaving me in a state of shock. Despite my careful precautions using birth control, the reality of an unplanned pregnancy still hit me, leaving me grappling with emotions I wasn't ready to confront.

Shock gripped me first, followed swiftly by a wave of sadness. I had fought tirelessly to create a better life for my son and myself, yet in an instant, everything I had built felt as if it were crumbling beneath me. Frustration bubbled inside me, an unbearable heat rising in my chest. How could I let this happen? I clenched my fists, biting back tears, ashamed that despite my best efforts, I had ended up right where I swore I'd never be again.

When I told my child's father, I wasn't sure what his reaction would be. His face was unreadable—neither frustrated nor happy. But what could we do? This was happening, and we had to prepare for it together. For a while, only the two of us knew about the pregnancy. I kept it to myself, not ready to share the weight of the news with anyone else. I didn't know how to process it myself, let alone explain it to others. All I knew was that this was another challenge I had to face, and I wasn't sure how I was going to handle it.

Three weeks after discovering I was pregnant, a relentless wave of nausea crashed over me, worse than when I was pregnant with my first son. The acid taste of bile burned my throat as I hunched over the sink, my stomach twisting violently. Even the faintest whiff of food sent shivers down my spine, forcing me to retreat to my bed in exhaustion.

It wasn't until a month later that I went to the doctor to do my first ultrasound to find out how many months pregnant I was. I waited patiently as the doctor prepared me to perform the ultrasound.

Finally it was time to see my baby for the first time. I stared at the ultrasound screen, trying to process the blurry image in front of me. The silence in the room stretched, thick with anticipation. My heart raced as the doctor's voice cut through the stillness: You're having... twins. The words echoed in my mind, leaving me breathless and in shock, and I broke down in tears right there and then.

Shame washed over me instead of joy, deeper than it had before. I was twenty, about to have three children, and all I felt was frustration and disappointment. I detested my life, my decisions, and most of all, the sense of perpetual disappointment that ensnared me. I was truly on the verge of becoming just another teen mom statistic.

I wanted to scream at myself for being so careless, for letting this happen, but all I could do was sit in the silence, tears soaking my pillow.

Alicia Whyle

As days passed by after finding out I was carrying twins, I was more agitated than before, not only because of the physical toll but also because it made me miss work. I called my supervisor to explain my situation and request a week's sick leave, which she granted. But even after a week of rest, I knew it wasn't going to be enough. I was terrified, remembering how difficult my pregnancy with my son had been, and now I was facing the same challenges again—but this time, with two babies.

When my sick leave ended, I tried to return to work. However, halfway to the office, I would have to turn back because I felt too weak and kept vomiting. After three failed attempts, I ended up losing my job. My supervisor was understanding, giving me multiple chances, but the morning sickness just wouldn't settle. I felt defeated. The disappointment weighed on me heavily, and I couldn't hold back the tears.

The regret was suffocating, a constant reminder that I couldn't seem to get anything right. Losing my job—the first real job I had ever cared about—felt like another failure I couldn't recover from. I thought about the future and wondered how I was going to keep everything together and care for three children without a job.

Yet, in the midst of all that pain, a small thought crossed my mind: If God had brought me this far, could there still be a purpose in all of this? I didn't know the answer, but deep down, I knew I had to stay strong for my son. I had to find a way to cope with everything happening to me. Even though the weeks did not get any easier, I had to tell myself that I survived pregnancy and hardships before, and somehow I will find a way to do it again.

CHAPTER FIVE

Educational Pursuits

Bringing twins into the world should have been a beautiful new chapter, since most women dream about having twins, but instead, it felt like stepping into chaos. My relationship with my children's father became unpredictable, shifting between moments of support and distance. And now, with two newborns depending on us, the strain only intensified. While the delivery itself was smoother than my first, the reality of raising twins was anything but easy.

Beyond the Tears

Raising my children became a full-time responsibility. Every moment was filled with the demands of my children's needs, leaving me exhausted as I attempted to balance everything. When their father was at work, I was alone with their endless needs—feeding, changing, and soothing—only for the cycle to restart moments later. Even when he was home, the demands never truly lessened. And in the midst of it all, my eldest still needed my attention. There was no pause button, no time to catch my breath. Days blurred into nights, and rest became something I could only dream about.

I tried my best to hold everything together, but the constant crying—both theirs and mine—echoed through the small apartment like a haunting melody. The financial stress felt like a heavy weight on my shoulders, with each overdue bill reminding me how hard it was to stay afloat.

Alicia Whyle

No matter how much I gave, it never felt like enough—never enough money, never enough time, never enough of me to go around.

Some nights, when the babies finally drifted off, I'd sit in the dim glow of the kitchen light, my head in my hands, tears slipping down my cheeks. Is this what motherhood is supposed to feel like? The exhaustion wasn't just physical; it seeped into my bones, making even the simplest tasks feel like mountains I didn't have the strength to climb.

Eventually, I began to worry about myself. The sadness wasn't just lingering—it was settling in, taking root like an unwelcome guest. The exhaustion was more than just lack of sleep—it left me feeling drained and unable to think clearly.

One morning, as I caught my reflection in the mirror, I barely recognized the hollow eyes staring back at me. My once-bright gaze was dull, my skin sallow, my body moving through the motions of life without truly living. What's wrong with me?

Desperate for answers, I turned to the internet. Late at night, with my babies nestled in their cribs, I scrolled through endless articles until I found it. The words postpartum depression blinked back at me, and suddenly, the chaos in my mind had a name. It wasn't just exhaustion, and it wasn't that I was failing as a mother. I wasn't alone in this. Finally, everything I was feeling made sense.

Attract Who You Want To BE

Knowing what I was facing didn't fix everything overnight, but it gave me something I hadn't felt in a long time—peace of mind.

As time passed, my children's father made the difficult decision to quit his job, saying the pressure had become unbearable. Even though I knew it would make things harder for us, I supported him, hoping he would find something better soon. However, as the days dragged into weeks, the reality of our situation felt like a heavy burden on my shoulders.

He tirelessly sought a stable job, but the doors continued to close. He took on small private jobs whenever he could, but there was no steady paycheck, no guarantee that we'd make it through the month. Meanwhile, our funds were running dangerously low, and the children's needs never stopped growing.

The pressure was relentless. Some days, I stared at the near-empty tin of formula, wondering how I would stretch it for one more feeding. Other nights, I held my babies close, their tiny bodies wrapped in makeshift cloth diapers because we had no money for more. The guilt gnawed at me. What kind of mother was I if I couldn't even provide the basics?

It got so bad that his great-grandmother, out of love and quiet desperation, would secretly take diapers meant for another great-grandchild just to give to us. I felt grateful but ashamed—ashamed that we had to depend on the kindness of an old woman to keep our babies clean, ashamed that no matter how hard we tried, we were still drowning.

The stress, once a distant hum, slowly crept into every corner of our relationship, like a storm gathering strength. It started with cold silences and bitter words thrown like daggers, but it didn't stop there. The verbal blows escalated, and soon physical ones followed. Every hit felt like a small piece of me was chipped away—my strength, my confidence, my sense of self. I was breaking, but I stayed, clinging to the hope that things would change. For two long years, I pretended, convincing myself I could fix what was falling apart. But the pretending was exhausting, and the pain... unbearable. It felt like things were slowly getting worse, with each day adding more to the fire.

The thought of leaving my children without their father was unbearable, but staying felt just as dangerous, as I feared he might take my life. I had tried everything—prayed, pleaded, sacrificed—but the love that once filled our home was now a hollow echo.

When the final blow came, it didn't surprise me. My heart shattered, and in that moment, I knew that the only way forward was to walk away, no matter how much it hurt. The choice was no longer about saving a relationship—it was about saving myself.

Even though my heart was broken, I knew I couldn't give up on myself because doing so would be equivalent to giving up on my children.

Fighting Against the Odds

Now that I was alone, with little physical or financial support, the struggle was relentless. But the interviewer's words kept echoing in my mind—her advice to go back to school, reminding me just how crucial those CXC passes were. That realization weighed heavily on me, igniting a sense of urgency I couldn't ignore.

Financially, full-time schooling was unattainable; however, I was determined not to let my circumstances dictate the outcome. I'd spent so much time making excuses—now it was time to fight back. That's when I made the decision. I wasn't going to wait for the 'perfect moment.' I had to act. With a heart full of fierce determination, I made my way to the Ministry of Education to pay and sign up for three CXC exams. There I made a promise to myself. I committed to persevere and reclaim my future, regardless of the length or difficulty of the journey.

Since I could not attend any institute for classes, I resolved to stay home, study, and teach myself. I envisioned the day I would finally hold those exam results in my hands, a tangible affirmation of my hard work and perseverance. This time, I was ready to embrace the challenges ahead and fight for the opportunities I had longed for.

I was extremely excited as I delved back into my books. There was a thrill in the air, a sense of achievement that surged through me as I embraced this new journey. Every page I turned felt like a step toward my future, rekindling a dormant passion for learning. The anticipation of studying subjects that once seemed daunting filled me with hope and determination.

Finally, the day of my exams arrived, filled with a mixture of nerves and excitement. Knowing how much depended on my performance, I poured all my energy and determination into those test papers. I felt a weight lift off my shoulders as I exited the exam room, but a fresh wave of anticipation swept over me— would I pass? I couldn't help but replay each question in my mind, wondering if I had done enough.

The waiting period felt endless, with each day dragging on as I anxiously awaited the results. Though my mind was filled with potential outcomes, I secretly harbored the belief that my efforts were sufficient. Finally, after years of dreaming, the moment inevitably came—the day I received my CXC passes. It was not my full CXC certificate, but it was a start. When the results came in, my heart raced as I opened the envelope. The grades were better than I expected. I had passed! Within that moment, a rush of relief and joy flooded over me.

I had fought so hard for this, and the feeling of holding those results in my hands was indescribable. Passing these exams wasn't just a goal; it was also about demonstrating to myself that I could overcome challenges and achieve even greater things.

Chasing the Dream a Second Time

Earning my CXC passes was a victory, a long-awaited achievement that reflected my determination. Yet, as I looked ahead, I realized that this was only the beginning. Despite my significant progress, the three subjects I pursued were insufficient to unlock the opportunities I required. The jobs they qualified me for barely paid enough to survive, let alone build the future I envisioned for my family. I had made progress, but I wasn't where I needed to be. I knew I had to keep pushing—to find a way to truly break free from the cycle that held me back.

With the excitement of learning ignited within me, I felt a powerful drive to dive deeper into my studies. My desire to achieve more blazed brightly, but the harsh reality of my finances kept intruding, reminding me of the limitations I faced. And so, I made the decision to start looking for a job.

Alicia Whyle

I eventually secured a position at a retail store, earning slightly more than minimum wage. It wasn't much, but it was a step in the right direction—a chance to provide for my three boys with a little more stability. With their father hardly present, the burden of responsibility fell entirely on my shoulders. Every dollar earned meant food on the table, clothes on their backs, and a small sense of security in a world that often felt unpredictable.

But even as I worked, a quiet restlessness remained. Providing for my children was my top priority, but deep down, I knew survival wasn't enough—I wanted more. The idea of returning to school still lingered in my mind, though it seemed impossible given my circumstances.

A woman I knew saw my struggles and how difficult life was for me. She encouraged me to visit a spiritual man who, she claimed, could take all my problems away. She explained that he would need to perform rituals and told me how much I would have to pay. Desperate to change my circumstances, I listened.

I went to his house, where his spiritual shop was located. As I sat outside, I felt ashamed and defeated. Around me were others just like me—people desperate for change, clinging to any hope they could find. But something in my spirit didn't feel right.

Right then and there, I started talking to God. I remember that conversation clearly. I said, "God, I am not going in to see that man. I'm leaving this place because deep down, I know this is wrong. I'm trusting you to take care of everything for me."

In that moment, I got up and walked away. Letting go and allowing God to take control transformed my life in ways I never expected. It was the best decision I had ever made, and in that very moment, everything began to change for me.

A few weeks later, on my way to work, I crossed paths with an old friend. As we talked, I found myself confiding in him, sharing my intense desire to go back to school—a dream that felt distant, yet lingered with a mix of hope and desperation. To my surprise, he listened intently and, without hesitation, offered to cover my tuition. I could hardly believe it. In that moment, gratitude flooded over me, mingled with a cautious disbelief. Was this my chance to rewrite my story? For the first time in a long while, success felt reachable. I was getting another chance to obtain all my CXC subjects.

After all the struggles of being a single working mom of three, my life took a positive turn when I least expected it. Just when I least expected it, God began to open doors I never imagined. He saw me as someone He loved, despite everything I had done in my life. When I was at my lowest, heartbroken, and in pain, He intervened and fulfilled one of my deepest desires.

Alicia Whyle

With excitement bubbling inside me, I eagerly began searching for schools to enroll in. After some research, I found one nearby that offered the exact classes I was interested in, which felt like a perfect fit. However, at 22, with three young children at home, the thought of sitting in a classroom full of teenagers felt daunting. I wrestled with the idea, questioning whether I could truly fit in—whether I was making the right decision.

But deep down, I knew this was bigger than my pride or discomfort. When I first walked into the private school to sign up, a surge of excitement mixed with nerves rushed through me. Just stepping through those doors felt like reclaiming a part of myself—a chance to prove that I was more than just a teenage mother who got pregnant at sixteen. I was capable of more.

During the registration process, the headmistress became aware of my age. Without hesitation, she extended a simple yet profoundly meaningful offer: I was given permission to wear regular clothes instead of the school uniform.

But even as I felt a deep gratitude for her understanding, I couldn't bring myself to reveal my personal life. I kept my children and the fact that I had been a teenage mom hidden. The weight of that shame still clung to me, a silent shadow I couldn't shake. I know it was unfair to my son to hide him away as if he was a mistake, but I feared being judged, labeled, and defined by my past. So, I stayed quiet, holding onto the opportunity she offered, hoping that this fresh start would allow me to leave those judgments behind and focus on building the future I desperately wanted.

The Sacrifice for Success

On the first day of school, I stepped through the gates, determined to embrace this second chance with everything I had. After years of reflecting on my pain and struggles, I had made a firm decision: I would not allow distractions to derail me. My mindset had shifted—I wasn't just attending school; I was reclaiming my future. This opportunity was too important to waste. I experienced a revitalized sense of purpose and was ready to dedicate myself fully.

At school, I intentionally distanced myself from people who wouldn't contribute to my growth, seeking out friends who would challenge me to be better. But ironically, I found myself becoming the one who encouraged others to strive for more. Perhaps this was due to my extensive life experience and direct observation of the challenges faced by those without formal education.

As I pursued my education this time, I was fully committed. I threw myself into my studies, determined to make up for all the time I had lost. My goal was clear: to walk out of that school with the grades I desired to move forward. Every moment mattered. There was no room for mistakes, no second-guessing. I knew I had to succeed—there was no other option for me.

I was no longer the teenage girl I once was; I had evolved into a young woman, forged by struggles that had forced me to grow up faster than anyone could imagine. Life had tested me in ways most people my age would never truly understand. However, I was determined to break the cycle of poverty that had caught my family and extended relatives.

The past year had tested me in ways I never imagined. The pressure of my responsibility felt constant, with every day seeming like a battle. Juggling school and caring for my kids was exhausting, but I couldn't stop. Mornings were always chaotic—getting everyone ready for daycare and school while trying to keep myself together. I couldn't afford a stroller, so I carried both of my boys in my arms, walking the fifteen-minute stretch to daycare. My arms ached with each step, but I pushed through. After dropping them off, I'd catch a ride to school, fighting exhaustion as I tried to stay focused through hours of lectures.

I was truly enjoying school in a way I never had before. The excitement of learning felt new and exhilarating, and I was so focused I didn't want to miss a single thing. My dedication didn't go unnoticed. Teachers recognized my effort and started offering extra help, ensuring I had what I needed to succeed. For the first time, I felt surrounded by people who believed in me and my potential.

After a long day of classes, I couldn't wait to pick up my little ones. Then the evening routine began: cooking dinner, helping with homework, cleaning up, and settling them into bed. I was doing it all alone, with no one to offer a break. Despite the exhaustion, every hug and smile from my kids reminded me why I kept going.

Too worn out to study after all that, I'd bathe and collapse into bed, craving a moment of peace. But I knew I had to sacrifice if I wanted to succeed, so I set my alarm for 2 a.m. Waking up in the silence of the night, I'd gather my notes and dive into my homework. Each moment felt heavy, but I pushed through, believing that my efforts would pay off.

After a few hours of studying, I'd go back to sleep until 6 a.m. It was a tough routine, but I reminded myself that this effort was for my children. Every hour spent studying was a step toward achieving my goal. My days revolved around school, and every spare moment I had was split between spending precious time with my children and poring over my books.

Alicia Whyle

This routine became my life, driven by a desire to create a brighter tomorrow for us all. Every challenge I faced only fueled my determination. I was no longer waiting for life to give me a break—I was taking control, one lesson at a time.

CHAPTER SIX

Soaring Beyond Limits

As I advanced in my educational journey, I knew this was my moment. I had faced countless challenges, but now, I was ready to rise. I couldn't forget where I came from, but I was committed to taking control of where my life was headed. As time passed, my friend who paid for my schooling evolved into more than just a friend; he became a tremendous support and a constant source of strength.

Whenever I felt like I couldn't push through, he was there, reminding me to keep going. His encouragement was always motivating, positive, and uplifting.

On the hardest days, when the weight of it all felt unbearable, he would pray with me, helping to ease the burden, even if just for a moment. He was a constant voice, reminding me that I could overcome anything as long as I kept pushing forward.

It was that unwavering support that fueled my determination, even when others couldn't understand it. My math teacher could not understand why I was so persistent, always tackling the problem no matter how many times I failed. Surely, she would never understand unless she had been through what I had. I felt like this was my last opportunity to reclaim my education, that it would never come around again. So, I remained persistent, highly motivated, and determined to succeed.

Despite everything, my sacrifices enabled me to excel in school, my determination shining through my circumstances. Every morning, I walked into that classroom with a fiercely confident attitude, ready to conquer whatever lay ahead. I worked hard, pushing myself to the top of my classes, earning not only excellent grades but also the admiration of my teachers, who recognized my relentless spirit and motivation.

In those moments of achievement, I felt a joy that confirmed I was heading in the right direction. Each small victory, like acing my weekly tests, fueled my passion to keep moving forward.

The Gift of Help

As the exams drew closer, just a few weeks before, our mathematics tutor unexpectedly left, abandoning the syllabus halfway through. I felt a wave of dread wash over me—math was already such a difficult subject, and now it seemed we were all set up to fail. But I couldn't allow myself to give in. I needed to pass; I had already sacrificed so much to get to this point.

In that moment of uncertainty, I found myself walking through the library one afternoon when I came across a group of teenagers deeply immersed in their math textbooks.

Knowing that I was much older than them, I swallowed my pride and approached them, desperately asking if they could help me with mathematics. To my relief, they said yes. I pulled up a chair, my nerves tingling with both gratitude and doubt.

I humbled myself, absorbing every word, formula, and concept they imparted to me. That group of teenagers opened doors in my mind I hadn't even realized were there, helping me grasp ideas that once seemed impossible. I met with them on numerous occasions, and over time, they taught me everything I needed to know to complete the syllabus. I was now sure that I was prepared to pass mathematics.

At that moment I experienced the truth that when God says it's your time to win, you cannot lose, no matter what circumstances are thrown your way.

The next year finally arrived, bringing with it the moment I had been working so hard for—my exams were here. As I walked into the exam room, a sting of anticipation washed over me. Sitting there, it felt almost surreal. I glanced down at the questions and knew that I was ready.

Gratitude swelled within me as I answered each question, thankful to God for this opportunity and to my friend for helping me get to this point. Without them, I would not have been in this room, writing these exams. As I finished each test paper, a sense of joy and satisfaction blossomed in my heart.

Attract Who You Want To BE

As the months passed by, I waited anxiously for my results, even though I was confident I did well. Then, the day finally arrived. With trembling hands, I opened my results, bracing myself. As my eyes scanned the page, I could hardly breathe. I had done it. I had passed all my exams with high grades. I was so proud of myself. Despite the warnings about how difficult these exams would be, here was the proof—when you believe in yourself and put in the work, you can achieve anything.

A rush of fulfillment filled every corner of my heart. I had dreamed of this, fought for it, and now, it was real. Tears of joy sprang to my eyes as I realized just how far I'd come. This wasn't just success; it was a victory over every doubt, every setback, and everything I had faced. And in that moment, I felt truly unstoppable.

After everything I'd endured, for the first time, I truly felt like an empowered young woman. I no longer had to pretend to be educated; I now held the tangible proof in my hands. It was as though a new world had opened up before me, full of possibilities I hadn't dared to imagine before.

Fueled by newfound confidence, I was determined to keep pushing forward. These results proved that I was capable of even greater achievements, and it was time to take my education to the next level.

I had achieved a significant milestone in my life by becoming qualified to enroll in any diploma program I desired. The word qualified resonated deeply within me; I wanted to demonstrate to all those who looked down on me that I was capable of more than what this world had labeled me to be. My emotions were releasing forth pride, relief, and disbelief at the same time. The path had been grueling, filled with so many obstacles, but here I was, standing at a turning point I had once thought impossible.

I have always been fascinated by computers, so I immediately enrolled in a diploma program at an institute to study Business Information Systems, delving into a field that felt like a true calling.

Key Achievements on My Journey

Every milestone I achieved represents a triumph over obstacles and a step toward success. Balancing education, family, and personal growth was no simple feat, but each victory reinforced my determination to rise above life's challenges.

At 24, I earned seven CXC passes—a moment that once felt unreachable. After the setbacks of early motherhood, self-doubt had clouded my dreams, but this achievement reignited my confidence.

By 25, I completed my first diploma in computer studies, a moment that brought tears to my eyes. Determined to keep pushing forward, I went on to earn my second diploma at 26.

That same year, my life took a beautiful turn—I married my friend, the one who supported me through it all. I remember the emotions washing over me as I walked down the aisle, my heart pounding in my chest. My boys, looking dashing in their navy blue suits, walked beside the flower girls, who looked like golden princesses.

There he stood at the altar in an ivory suit with a gold inner shirt, his eyes filled with love and excitement as he waited for me. I felt like Cinderella, stepping into a dream, adorned in a white ball gown with delicate lace appliqués and shimmering rhinestones. Tears welled in my eyes as I took each step, knowing that I was about to begin a new life with a man who truly loved and believed in me.

But life didn't stop there. At 26, balancing my studies, family, and responsibilities as a wife and mother left me feeling extremely exhausted. My job, which once seemed like a stable option, no longer fit into the time I needed to dedicate to my education and my family. But I refused to accept that as my reality. I knew I had to take control of my situation before everything began to fall apart. Using the knowledge I had gained so far in my business studies, I made the bold decision to start my own business. With unshakable determination and the guidance of the Holy Spirit, I built my bridal boutique from the ground up.

It wasn't just about making money—it was about proving to myself that I could take action, adapt, and rise above the circumstances when one path wasn't working. I didn't wait for things to change; I made the change happen.

At 27, I earned my advanced diploma and entered into my final year in the degree program.

Through it all, I've discovered that it doesn't matter what your past looked like—what matters is refusing to make excuses and instead making the right choices and sacrifices to shape your future. With faith, even the most difficult times can become opportunities for greatness.

As I entered the final year of my degree program, I was excited to be drawing closer to my goal. Because of my impressive qualifications, I now had the freedom to choose where to complete my final year without limitations. This was a moment of triumph—a privilege I had once only dreamed of a few years ago.

I no longer wanted to remain at my previous institution; therefore, after careful consideration, I applied to the University of Herefordshire in London, where I studied Business Administration. A month after applying, my acceptance letter arrived. The moment I opened it, my heart melted. Tears streamed down my face as I grasped the weight of this achievement. Coming from a family where no one had ever attended university, this wasn't just an acceptance—it was a breakthrough, a defiance of generational odds.

The Final Stretch

The journey to completing my degree was truly a test of endurance. My lecturers introduced themselves to me and the courses I will be taking. It felt like stepping into a new, intimidating world, but by the second and third classes, I found myself captivated. Modules like Marketing, International Human Resource Management, and Contemporary Issues in Business Management quickly became favorites. But then came the first major challenge: my Global Marketing and Ethics assignment.

As someone accustomed to traditional exams, assignments presented a new challenge. I had no idea where to begin, and the looming deadlines felt like insurmountable walls. This assignment

Alicia Whyle

was so difficult that I found myself on the verge of giving up. This was not like my diploma exams; this was on a much more difficult level. It was during one of these low moments that my husband sat me down. His words were simple but impactful: "You've come too far to give up now. Will you quit the next one too? So I kept moving and researching, trying to find ways to finish the assignment, and eventually I did.

By the end of the first semester, I had successfully completed all my assignments and passed every module. It was a tremendous relief, as I had doubted continuously whether I would make it. Encouraged by this achievement, I excitedly set a new goal—to graduate with first-class honors.

As I approach my final semester, the final stretch was anything but smooth. As the last two modules approached, everything hinged on their results. A single grade could determine whether I achieved my goal for First Class honors or not. My heart sank when I received a B for one module. I knew this meant the odds of first-class honors were slipping away. I couldn't sleep, and I couldn't eat. I felt like I was about to fall short of achieving my goals. My thoughts were filled with hypothetical scenarios. I knew I could not go on this way, so I sought counseling from a pastor I once knew. He encouraged me and helped me to calm my thoughts using the word of God.

But the road ahead was still argonizing. The remaining module would require an impossibly high score to balance my grades—something rarely achieved at that university. Desperation turned into prayer. I clung to the words of a Christian radio announcer: "If you need the impossible, call on the God of the impossible." And so I did. I prayed earnestly, asking for an extremely high score in this module.

The day I received the results was one of the most nerve-wracking moments of my life. As I opened the grade report online, at first I was afraid to look at it. When I finally got the courage to open it and look at the score, I screamed so loud in excitement. Not only had I achieved the required grade, but I had also set a record for the highest mark in the university's history. My paper was chosen as a model for future students. Tears streamed down my face as I reflected on what I had accomplished—I was now the proud owner of a first-class honors degree. Yep, that's me—a teen mom who surpassed most of the students in my class, many of whom had no responsibilities like mine, who didn't even have a child.

At the age of 22, I made the bold decision to return to school, fully aware that the road ahead would be long and interesting. Now, at 28, I've completed my degree. I did it. Despite facing sleepless nights, balancing school, motherhood, and everything in between, I never gave up.

Alicia Whyle

These weren't just academic milestones; they were hard-fought victories, each one a testament to the struggles I faced and conquered. This served as evidence of how far I had come and how far I was willing to go to change my story.

With every battle won, I moved closer to the moment that would change everything—the day I would finally stand in my cap and gown, proof that every struggle had been worth it.

PART 3
TRANSFORMATION & TRIUMPH

CHAPTER SEVEN

The Pinnacle Moment

Three months had passed since I received my degree results, and the day I had been waiting for since I had my son was just one week away. It was graduation time. For days, I couldn't stop thinking about the ceremony. It was a moment that meant so much to me, not just because it marked the culmination of years of hard work, but also because it was a milestone I'd never had the chance to experience.

A Dream Realized

As time drew closer to graduation, the excitement going through me was indescribable. I was meticulous about every detail. The dress, the shoes, the hairstyle, the accessories—every detail had to be flawless. That ceremony presented me with the opportunity to shine, and I wanted everything to be flawless.

Finally the day for my graduation arrived. As I looked in the mirror, I couldn't help but smile at my reflection, and for once in years, I loved it. I saw a woman who had faced numerous setbacks, endured extreme challenges, and persevered to reach the end. My husband, constantly by my side, was there to accompany me. His words of pride and support meant the world to me. "I'm so proud of you," he said, and in that moment, I realized how much he had invested in my journey. Still, he was there through every late-night study session and self-doubt. He had believed in me when I struggled to believe in myself.

But amidst all the joy and excitement, a part of me couldn't shake the sadness that lingered in my heart. My mother wasn't there. I had invited her to come, but she told me she could not make it.

This broke my heart because, deep down, I knew she could have made it if she wanted to. I wanted so badly for her to be there because I thought for a moment she could witness my transformation and be proud of me. My heart yearned for her forgiveness and love for so long, especially knowing how deeply my actions had hurt her when I got pregnant at sixteen.

The shame and disappointment I brought into her life seemed to linger, no matter how hard I tried, as if nothing I did could ever erase them. I had hoped that my achievements over the years would be enough to speak for me, to show her that I wasn't defined by that teenage pregnancy. Despite everything, I had transformed into a person worth believing in. But deep down, I feared it would never be enough for her to truly see me.

However, I couldn't let her absence overshadow what I had worked so hard for. I had to savor the moment— my moment..

Owning the Stage

As I put on my gown and prepared to join the other graduates, I was filled with emotion. My heart was humbled with gratitude. I couldn't stop smiling—this moment felt like a dream, and I couldn't believe it was finally happening to me. The walk down the aisle, alongside my fellow graduates, felt amazing.

Attract Who You Want To BE

Each step was filled with a mixture of emotions. I could feel my tear glands starting to tingle. This was actually happening to me. I felt the floodgates threatening to open, but I fought to hold it together. As I looked around, seeing the proud faces of lecturers and friends filled me with a profound sense of appreciation for how far God has brought me.

Walking across that stage, though, was like nothing I had ever experienced. The moment I stepped forward, the world seemed to slow down so I could shine. When the announcer called my name and I stepped onto the stage to receive my degree, my heart was pounding with nervousness. Hearing "First Class Honours" felt like the weight of all the struggles, sacrifices, sleepless nights, and self-doubt I had carried for so long finally lifting off my shoulders. I stood there, a living testament to my own resilience, proving to myself and to everyone who doubted me that I was capable of far more than they ever imagined.

Among this outstanding achievement, I was also honored with two awards—one for earning a first-class honors degree and another for achieving the highest score in that last module. What an awesome day it was—everything I imagined it to be and more.

And now, as I looked at the degree in my hands, I realized that I had fought for something no one could ever take away from me—my independence. It was more than just a credential; it was a foundation, a key to unlocking new opportunities and shaping the future I had always envisioned.

Graduation marked the end of self-doubt and the beginning of a new belief in myself. For years, I had struggled with insecurity, questioning whether I was worthy of success or capable of achieving anything meaningful. However, this day marked a pivotal moment in my life. The pride I felt as I walked across that stage wasn't just about the degree or the awards; it was about silencing all the voices that had ever told me I wasn't good enough. I had confronted my fears, doubts, and past, emerging stronger and more confident than ever before.

That day I walk away as one of the top students in that year. This accomplishment didn't just change how I saw myself—it also had the power to inspire others. As I stood with my degree, I thought about the other young women, single mothers, and those who were told they would mount down to nothing good. If they could see me standing on that stage despite everything I had been through, maybe they'd believe that they could do it too. Perhaps they could see that no matter the obstacles, no matter the doubts, they could rise above it all and achieve their own dreams.

When God says it's your time to win, nothing can stop you—not even the struggles or the setbacks. Throughout my six years of studies, I did not have to repeat any of my exams or assignments.

Attract Who You Want To BE

God's timing is flawless, and when He says it's your moment, you can't lose.

CHAPTER EIGHT

Rise Above The Ashes

Becoming a mother at a young age brought its own set of struggles; I encountered challenges so daunting that not all of them can be captured in this book. However, I'll share some of the most significant struggles I faced and how I overcame them. Through each trial, I discovered strength I never knew I had and learned that transformation begins when you embrace your story, no matter how hard it may seem, and take action. Each struggle shaped me, molded my character, and, ultimately, empowered me to become the woman I am today.

Challenges Faced

Low Self-Esteem: My self-esteem reached its lowest point when I became pregnant. I felt like a complete failure, a disappointment to everyone who cared for me. It was as if every negative word spoken over my life by my grandmother and others had taken root and begun to bloom. I started to believe I was incapable of greatness, that my dreams were no longer within reach.

I hated my reflection. My belly stretched and scarred, my breasts no longer sat the way they used to, and I felt like I had lost the right to be seen as beautiful. I once overheard a man say, "She is attractive, but she simply needs to lose those love handles." I was barely 115 pounds—what love handles was he even talking about? But because I already felt insecure about my body, his words stuck with me. They fed into the self-doubt I was already battling, making me question my worth even more. I did not value myself because I saw nothing within me that was beautiful, and the world sure made that clear.

I had no confidence. No education. Nothing that made me feel worthy. When I stood beside other women, I shrank inside, convinced they were better than me in every way. I wasn't just struggling with self-doubt—I was drowning in it. But I knew that if I didn't take action, I would remain stuck in that cycle.

I faced my self-doubt head-on by taking deliberate steps to address the things that I hated about myself. The first change I made was physical: I committed to exercising at the gym, determined to firm up my belly and slim my waistline. It wasn't just about appearance—it was about reclaiming control over my body and convincing myself that I was beautiful. Alongside this, I began using creams to improve the elasticity of my skin, working to reduce the stretch marks that had long been a source of insecurity.

But physical changes alone weren't enough. I knew I had to nourish my mind as well. I poured through school books, determined to sharpen my intellect until I could fully enroll in school. I needed to prove to myself that I was more than the doubts that had plagued me. Along the way, I also reminded myself of the things I loved about who I was—my ambitious spirit, my deep love for God, and yes, the beauty I saw in my own face.

The most profound shift came when I joined a mentorship program, where I learned to see myself through a lens of love and acceptance, grounded in the eyes of God. It was there I realized that true confidence isn't about perfection; it's about embracing who you are, flaws and all, and seeing yourself as worthy of love and greatness.

Social Judgment: The social judgment I faced was relentless. People called me names I did not even know exsisted. Even some of my relatives ridiculed me for becoming pregnant at 16, offering no compassion or support. Everyone I encountered who knew I got pregnant at that age judged me, and that's why I kept it hidden when I encountered new persons. I wanted to prove them all wrong. There were times when I felt ashamed to walk down the road because I was never sure who I would encounter. I can't remember one person in my village who was compassionate about my situation.

However, there came a time when I was determined to overcome the criticism and demonstrate to everyone that, even though I became pregnant at sixteen, my son and I could still achieve greatness. I took back control of my future by returning to school, dedicating myself to my studies, and surrounding myself with people who believed in me.

Those harsh words and criticisms ignited my drive to strive beyond my previous limits. They pushed me to stay focused, to dig deeper, and to work harder than I ever thought I could. I made the sacrifices needed—sacrifices that tested my limits—because I understood that the opportunities before me were too valuable to be wasted.

Every ounce of effort, every moment of discipline, was dedicated to ensuring that the chance I had been given wasn't squandered but rather fully utilized to secure my success.

With every step forward, I reminded myself that my story wasn't over—it was only beginning. I knew that one day, they would hear my story, and when they saw me, they would witness the undeniable truth that a greater force was working through me. And they did. I rose above the young people my age in that village. I became a first-class honors student and an entrepreneur, and my son attended one of the most prestigious secondary schools in my country.

This wasn't just about me—it was about showing them that one decision does not define the course of your future. God's grace is sufficient, and He can rewrite any story, just as He did mine.

Attract Who You Want To BE

Exhaustion: At my age, parenting was a daily challenge. There were moments when I felt trapped, suffocated by the never-ending responsibilities, and overwhelmed by the constant demands of my children. The exhaustion was relentless, and I sometimes questioned whether I had the strength to keep going. I felt like I had disappeared, like my own needs no longer mattered. My body ached from sleepless nights, my mind was heavy with worries, and my emotions swung between guilt and frustration.

But in the midst of that chaos, a realization struck me—if I didn't take time for myself, even in the smallest ways, I would eventually have a mental breakdown. I gave my children, responsibilities, and goals so much attention that I neglected my own well-being.

Eventually, I made a conscious decision to carve out moments just for me. Sometimes, my aunt would take the boys to church on a Saturday, and I used that time to rest—allowing myself to sleep without guilt, to breathe without pressure. I also started dedicating time during the week to simple acts of self-care. I would do facials at home, put on an exercise video to relieve tension, or even just unwind with a movie and my favorite ice cream.

More importantly, I learned to be intentional about showing myself love. Whether it was through meditation, quiet reflection, or just finding small pockets of time to relax, I embraced the fact that caring for myself wasn't selfish—it was necessary.

And as I nurtured my own well-being, I became a better mother—more relaxed, more patient, and truly present for my children.

Unstable Relationship: I once believed that the father of my children and I were inseparable, that our love was strong enough to withstand anything. But reality shattered that illusion when I became pregnant. The man I thought I knew changed before my eyes—his warmth faded, replaced by mood swings, aggression, and a lack of support when I needed him the most. What should have been a time of unity turned into a period of painful isolation.

The strain didn't just affect me; it weighed heavily on my children. They deserved a father's love, but he offered little—no emotional presence, no financial support. Eventually, he remarried, distancing himself even further. Court battles for child maintenance dragged on, but deep down, I knew I was fighting for something he had no interest in giving. The disappointment was devastating, and I was hurting inside beyond measure.

Instead of dwelling on his lack of provision, I resolved to overcome it. I poured my energy into my education and business, determined to create a life where my children would never feel the void of his absence. I worked tirelessly, ensuring they lacked nothing. Over time, I stopped chasing after what was never there. Accepting that their father had chosen to walk away was painful, but it motivated me even more. I built a future where they thrived, not as children of an absent father, but as children of a mother who refused to let them go without.

Limited Support System: One of the hardest challenges I faced as a mother was the lack of a support system. My family—my aunts, uncles, and even my own mother—treated me differently the moment I became pregnant. It was as if I had done something unforgivable, and instead of rallying around me, they abandoned me.

Aside from my aunt's small gestures on Saturdays, no one else offered to watch my boys so I could have a moment to breathe.

The isolation was painful. There were times when I longed for just a few hours to myself—to step away from the responsibilities, to feel like more than just a mother. However, each time I sought assistance, I encountered silence or justifications. Eventually I stopped asking because I understood where I stood in their eyes.

At first, for years, I didn't know how to cope. I simply did what I had to do—I carried my children with me everywhere. If I had an errand, they were right there beside me. Whenever I received an invitation, I would either accept it or bring them along. But as I grew older, I realized that while I couldn't change my family's response, I could change my situation.

When I started making money, I made it a priority to hire babysitters—people I could trust to care for my children while I took much-needed time for myself. I also found creative ways to bring balance into my life.

When I got married, I started putting the kids to bed early so my husband and I could create date nights at home, turning our living room into a romantic escape, ensuring that our relationship didn't suffer because of the lack of external support.

Looking back, I see that my struggle forced me to become resourceful. I learned the value of coming up with my own solutions when there were none available.

Financial Hardship: On certain days, I meticulously counted every dollar, making every effort to ensure my boys had everything they required. Every cent I received, no matter where it came from, went straight to their necessities—diapers, food, clothes, and transportation. There was barely anything left for me. I couldn't afford to get my hair done, buy simple cosmetics, or even treat myself to a movie for a brief escape from reality.

I always knew that having a good education was my way out. I returned to school, determined to acquire such advanced qualifications that no employer could reject me. I became overqualified for most of the positions I saw advertised in newspapers or on company websites.

Beyond that, I made another bold move—I started my own business. I wanted to ensure that financial hardship would never control my life again. With each step forward, I created opportunities that allowed me to not just survive but build a life where we could be truly comfortable.

Looking back, the sacrifices were worth it. My struggle triggered my ambition, and today, I stand as proof that determination can turn even the darkest situations into success.

Self-doubt in Parenthood: Who can truly ever fully prepare for motherhood? There were moments when I felt like I was failing, questioning whether I was doing it right. Some days, the tantrums, unnecessary crying, and endless fighting between my children felt akin to a third world war. I would find myself wondering what I was doing wrong. Was I too strict? Too lenient? Did they not like me because of the rushed, chaotic mornings or the constant need to discipline them?

Alicia Whyle

The exhaustion often came not just from the sleepless nights but from the emotional weight of their tears. Seeing them upset, even over the smallest things, made me question myself as a mother. There were moments when I genuinely wondered if my kids resented me, especially during their intense tantrums that left me feeling helpless and defeated. I wanted to do everything perfectly, but the reality of parenting was far from perfect.

Over time, I came to realize that motherhood is not about perfection—it's a continuous learning experience. There is no manual, no step-by-step guide that guarantees success. As they grew, I grew too. I learned to give myself grace, to understand that I didn't have to have it all figured out at once. Every challenge, every difficult moment, was an opportunity to learn and improve.

Parenting isn't about always knowing the answers; it's about showing up, learning as you go, and embracing the journey with love and patience. And as I let go of the pressure to be the perfect mother, I found peace in knowing that I was doing my best—and that was more than enough.

Rewards and Joys

Motherhood, despite its challenges, brought a joy I had never anticipated. My boys became my greatest source of light, their laughter and love filling even the darkest days. No matter how exhausted I felt, their hugs, their innocent questions, and the way they looked at me with admiration reminded me that every sacrifice was worth it.

One of the proudest moments of my life came when my firstborn, the son I had as a teenager, achieved something extraordinary. He topped his entire school in the SEA exam, scoring an impressive 98%. This earned him a place in one of the most prestigious schools in the country, completely free of charge. The news came just a year after I had graduated, making the moment even more perfect.

I vividly recall being outside his school on the day of the results announcement. The moment he saw me, he ran into my arms, his excitement overflowing. As I held him close, I whispered, "Yes, we did it, baby. You topped the school, and I topped the university. That moment was more than just an academic victory—it was proof that we had defied the odds. We were not statistics or failures. We had risen above every challenge, proving that a teenage pregnancy did not mean the end of a future but rather the start of a new, determined journey.

Alicia Whyle

His success was a result of our perseverance and sacrifices as well as his hard work. It was a victory we both shared, a testament to the fact that we are so much more than the labels others place upon us.

As I reflect on how far I've come and the victories I've achieved, I realize that none of this would have been possible without a shift in my mindset—a shift that allowed me to focus, overcome obstacles, and embrace my true potential.

Now, as I move forward, it's time to explore how developing a positive and focused mindset is key to attracting the life you desire.

PART 4

ATTRACTING THE LIFE YOU DESIRE

CHAPTER NINE

Shifting Your Mindset for Success

Attraction is more than just a mystical force or a stroke of luck—it is a reflection of who we are at our core. Every thought we nurture, every belief we hold, and every action we take shapes the energy we emit into the world. Attract Who You Want to Be is not just a concept; it is a transformative journey that challenges you to align your mindset, habits, and identity with the life you desire.

The truth is, we do not attract what we want—we attract what we are. If we carry self-doubt, we will find ourselves surrounded by situations and people that reinforce that reality. If we embody confidence and purpose, we will naturally draw opportunities that align with that energy.

Personal transformation is the bridge between where we are and where we want to be. When we change internally, everything around us begins to shift.

This section of the book will guide you through that transformation. You will discover how to reshape your mindset, redefine your identity, and attract a life that aligns with your highest potential.

Your Mindset Shapes Your Reality

For as long as I can remember, I've dreamed of being an independent woman—someone who could walk into a store and buy whatever she desired without hesitation. My vision of success was shaped by my favorite character, Toni Childs from Girlfriends. She was everything I longed to be: rich, classy, independent, and effortlessly sophisticated. She loved luxurious things and unapologetically pursued the finer things in life.

I wanted that life for myself. In contrast, in that same show, there was Maya Wilkes, the teenage mom who struggled financially. She could only shop at retail outlets and often had to decline invitations to luxurious dinner parties, unlike her other friends who could afford designer stores. She embodied everything I feared becoming. Yet, by twenty, I was a struggling mother of three, my reality far closer to Maya's than Toni's.

As I watched women my age build the life I longed for, I felt trapped, drowned in responsibilities. I'd see them in their sharp office attire, working in banks or corporate jobs, with a confidence that came with their success. Meanwhile, I was at home, surrounded by diapers and bottles, wondering how my life had drifted so far.

I aspired to be exceptional, to build a life where my children could gaze upon me with pride, knowing that their mother had overcome great challenges. However, I convinced myself I wasn't smart enough, capable enough, or deserving enough to succeed.

Attract Who You Want To BE

Those thoughts became my prison, reinforcing the very struggles I wanted to escape.

But then I realize wanting more wasn't enough—I had to believe it was possible. That was when the shift happened. I realized that as long as I continued seeing myself the way I had, I would stay stuck in the very life I was desperate to escape. For years, I'd been burdened by thoughts like, "You're not good enough" and "You'll amount to nothing." But everything changed when I shifted my mindset. I decided to believe in myself, replacing "I can't" with "I will."

I started to visualize the person I wanted to be. I began to picture her daily: she was an educated woman who walked with purpose, who provided for her children without struggle, one who was financially stable and had full control of her life.

The hardest part was believing it was possible when nothing in my life seemed to reflect that vision. I had to make a choice: stop focusing on where I was and start focusing on where I wanted to go. Instead of focusing on obstacles, I began to see opportunities.

Suddenly, the excuses I had leaned on before didn't hold weight anymore. I stopped feeling sorry for myself and started taking action toward becoming that woman.

Alicia Whyle

The Power of Thoughts, Words, and Actions

Our thoughts, words, and actions are not just fleeting occurrences—they are the building blocks of our reality. Our thoughts shape our beliefs about ourselves and the world, which affects our speech and behavior. When we repeatedly affirm negative thoughts, they form limiting beliefs that trap us in a cycle of self-doubt and inaction.

Negativity surrounded me growing up, and the harsh words from my past echoed in my mind. My grandmother often remarked, "The only thing good that is black is a pair of shoes," a statement about my skin color that deeply affected me. For years as a child, I struggled to pass exams in school, allowing those words to define who I was and what I believed I was capable of.

Conversely, positive thoughts empower us to take the necessary steps toward the life we desire. The words we speak reinforce our inner narrative. Words have the power to uplift, motivate, or hinder progress, so choosing language that affirms our potential is crucial.

There came a pivotal moment in my life where I learned to silence the negative voices. I learned to replace my negative thoughts with the truth of what God's Word says about me. Whenever a negative thought crept in, telling me I wasn't capable or didn't deserve better, I fought it with the truth. I reminded myself of God's promises: I possess the mind of Christ, and I am made fearfully and wonderfully.

Finally, our actions are the tangible expressions of our thoughts and words. Without action, even the most positive thoughts remain just that—thoughts. It is through consistent, aligned actions that we begin to manifest the reality we envision.

Aligning Thoughts With Actionable Steps

Having the right mindset is a powerful first step, but it's the actions we take that will determine the outcome we desire. Action serves as the bridge between where we are now and where we want to be. To create the life we desire, our actions must align with the thoughts we think and the words we speak.

This means taking deliberate steps that reinforce our vision. If we believe we are capable of success, we must act as though that belief is true—pursuing opportunities, setting goals, and making decisions that propel us forward. It's not enough to wait for opportunities to come to us; we must actively seek them out, even in the face of fear or uncertainty.

For instance, I had a goal to pursue my education but couldn't afford tuition. Instead of letting that stop me, I took action—signing up for the exams and committing to teaching myself. My bold step not only pushed me forward, but it also opened up an unexpected opportunity: a friend offered to cover my tuition, allowing me to attend school full-time. By aligning my thoughts with action, I created the space for the opportunity I needed to move closer to my goals.

Aligning our thoughts with actionable steps means breaking down our goals into manageable tasks, staying disciplined, and adjusting as needed. With each step forward, we create momentum, reinforcing the reality we want to manifest.

Your actions don't need to be huge at first. Sometimes it's as simple as starting your day with a prayer, asking God for direction, or saying no to distractions. Over time, those small changes begin to build momentum, and before you know it, you're not just imagining the person you want to be—you're becoming them.

Overcoming Self-Limiting Beliefs

One of the most powerful barriers we face in life is the self-limiting beliefs we hold about ourselves. These beliefs often stem from past experiences or external influences, and they can shape how we see our potential.

To overcome them, we must first identify and reframe these beliefs into empowering ones. For example, the belief that we are not incapable of achieving something or that our circumstances define our future can keep us stuck. But when we change the narrative in our minds and replace it with the truth of our strength and potential, we can take control of our lives. The key is to recognize that our beliefs don't define us; they are just thoughts, and we have the power to change them.

Acting Despite Fear or Doubt

Acting despite fear or doubt is one of the most transformative things we can do. It's easy to wait until we feel fully ready, but often, that moment never comes. The truth is, we are never fully ready, but acting anyway builds the courage we need to move forward. It's about starting before we feel completely confident—

trusting that the steps we take, no matter how small, will bring us closer to our goals.

I vividly recall the belief I had to relearn: the notion that, as a teenage mother, I had lost my opportunity for success. This belief weighed heavily on me for years, convincing me that higher education and personal fulfillment were beyond my reach. But one day, I made a decision to act despite my doubts. I enrolled in school, unsure of how I would juggle the responsibilities of motherhood and academics.

Ultimately, my diligent efforts yielded results as I graduated with first-class honors, securing the top spot in my class. It was proof that taking action even when you are unsure can lead you to unexpected success.

The Role of Faith and Purpose

Faith and purpose are powerful forces that can transform doubt into clarity and fear into action. When you align your desires with God's plan, you begin to understand that your journey isn't just about personal ambition—it's about fulfilling a higher calling. This alignment requires not just belief but action. True faith isn't passive; it's about trusting God's timing while taking deliberate steps toward your purpose, even when the outcome isn't guaranteed.

Stepping out in faith often means moving forward with the information provided even without possessing all the answers. It's trusting that every step you take, no matter how small, will lead you closer to the life God has designed for you. Doubts may arise, but when you're rooted in faith, those doubts become smaller in the face of a greater purpose. It's about believing that setbacks are setups for something bigger and that, in God's time, every effort will bear fruit.

I took a significant risk when I launched my bridal business. I had no experience, no capital, or formal knowledge of the industry—just a deep desire to become financially stable, provide better for my family, and still have time for myself. The idea seemed daunting at first, since I will be operating the business from my living room, which was not very spacious at the time. Fear whispered every reason why it might not work. But I chose to silence those doubts with prayer, seeking God's direction at every step.

With each prayer came clarity, and with clarity came action. I took deliberate steps forward, starting with research to understand the industry, networking with others who had more experience, and investing my time into bringing this vision to life.

Alicia Whyle

Opportunities I couldn't have planned for started to appear—connections were made, clients began to trust my vision, and while the rewards took time to materialize, they did. The success of my business became a testament to what happens when you have faith in your plans and take action. Faith isn't just about waiting—it's about moving forward with intention, even when the road ahead feels unclear.

CHAPTER TEN

Becoming Who You Want to Attract

Attraction isn't just about what you desire—it's about who you become. The life you want, the relationships you seek, and the opportunities you hope for are often reflections of your inner world. True transformation starts from within, and external success is simply an extension of the growth that happens internally. When you align your thoughts, beliefs, and actions with the version of yourself you aspire to be, you naturally attract the people and experiences that resonate with that energy.

Embodying the Person You Aspire to Be

Becoming the person you want to attract requires intentional action. It's not just about wishing for success, love, or fulfillment—it's about actively cultivating the qualities that align with those desires. If you want to attract ambition, you must embody discipline. If you desire respect, you must carry yourself with confidence and integrity. If you seek love, you must first love yourself wholeheartedly. Every choice you make, from self-talk to habits, should reflect the reality you want.

For Kiara, the journey to self-worth was anything but easy. She was stuck in a cycle of self-doubt, believing she wasn't worthy of the success she longed for. She would often say, "People like me don't get those kinds of opportunities. But when I introduced her to the principles of self-transformation, everything changed. Instead of waiting for life to improve, she started working on herself. She read books on personal growth, dressed for the job she wanted, and walked into every room with confidence. The more she invested in herself, the more her world shifted. Soon, she started attracting high-value opportunities—job offers, promotions, and connections with influential people. By changing her mindset and taking deliberate action, Kiara became a magnet for the life she once thought was out of reach.

Confidence, Resilience, and Self-Worth

True transformation begins the moment you choose to believe in yourself. Confidence, resilience, and self-worth are not innate qualities; they are cultivated through action, perseverance, and self-acceptance. Stepping outside your comfort zone and embracing challenges as opportunities for transformation are essential steps on the journey to personal growth.

Confidence is not something you wait to feel—it is something you build through experience. It grows each time you face discomfort and take action despite hesitation. The more you expose yourself to new challenges, the more familiar and manageable they become. Confidence flourishes when you trust yourself enough to move forward, even when the outcome is unknown.

But confidence alone isn't enough. **Resilience** is equally essential. Resilience is the ability to adapt and recover when faced with obstacles. It is forged through adversity, not ease. Every failure, rejection, or misstep is an opportunity to strengthen your character. Instead of allowing difficulties to define you, resilience encourages you to learn from them, adjust, and keep pushing forward. It is not about avoiding hardship but about developing the mental and emotional fortitude to withstand it.

At the heart of both confidence and resilience is **self-worth.** Self-worth is the foundation upon which confidence and resilience stand. It involves acknowledging that external validation, achievements, or others' approval do not determine your value. True self-worth comes from within, rooted in self-respect and self-acceptance. When you know your worth, you make decisions that align with your highest self, set healthy boundaries, and refuse to settle for less than you deserve.

Fear, hesitation, and unpredictability are natural, but they should not be barriers to growth. The key to transformation is to act despite discomfort. Each step forward, no matter how small, reinforces your belief in yourself. Over time, these intentional efforts create lasting change, turning fear into confidence, struggles into resilience, and self-doubt into unwavering self-worth.

Healing from Past Hurts

To become the person you desire to attract, you must also heal from the past. Every emotional wound, every bit of unresolved pain, and every unhealed hurt you carry within you reflects in the energy you project into the world. If you're still holding onto anger, resentment, or regret, you will attract situations and people that mirror those same energies. Healing, therefore, becomes a critical step in transforming yourself into the person who can not only manifest the life you want but also attract the relationships and opportunities that align with your true self.

Healing is not an abstract concept; it's an active decision to release the emotional baggage that may be blocking your path to success and fulfillment. It starts with the daily practice of forgiveness—not just toward others, but toward yourself. Forgiving yourself for past mistakes, for holding onto pain, and for not taking action sooner frees you to step into the life you deserve. When you consciously choose to heal from your past hurts, you begin to transform your inner world, which in turn changes how you show up in the world. You begin to radiate a different energy, one that is open to love, success, and joy.

Alicia Whyle

Implementing Daily Habits For Transformation

The power of daily habits cannot be overstated when it comes to personal transformation. Small, consistent actions are the foundation upon which lasting change is built. These seemingly insignificant moments, when accumulated over time, create a ripple effect that leads to profound shifts in our mindset, our environment, and, ultimately, the kind of people and opportunities we attract into our lives. Making daily choices, no matter how minor they may seem in the moment, is the key to becoming the person you want to attract.

Each day is an opportunity to take one small step toward becoming the person you envision. These daily habits—whether it's a morning routine of self-care, a commitment to learning something new, or a dedication to nurturing positive relationships—serve as actions that reinforce your growth and goals. It's not about waiting for a big moment of change but about consistently showing up for yourself in ways that gradually shape the life you want to create.

In the same way, by committing to small but consistent actions, you too can align yourself with the life and relationships you want to manifest. Transformation begins with the daily habits that reinforce the person you are becoming—and through those actions, you become a magnet to the opportunities and people that resonate with your growth.

How to Manifest Your Ideal Life

Becoming a mother—especially at a young age—can feel like stepping into a world filled with uncertainties. The weight of responsibility, the fear of judgment, and the overwhelming need to provide for your child can make it difficult to see beyond the struggles of today. But no matter where you are right now, you have the power to attract the life you want. This isn't about wishful thinking or waiting for circumstances to change—it's about stepping into the belief that you are capable of more and taking intentional steps toward the future you desire. Let's explore these essential steps to manifest the life you truly deserve.

Clarify Your Vision and Believe It's Possible

The journey to attracting the life you want begins with clarity. Clarity is the first step in defining exactly what you want for yourself and your child. Many teen moms get stuck in survival mode, focusing only on getting through each day. But if you don't take time to envision the future you want, you might wake up years later feeling stuck in the same cycle, living a life full of regret.

For most young mothers, the biggest challenge isn't just setting a vision—it's believing they can achieve it. Ask yourself: If nothing was holding you back, what kind of life would you create? Do you see yourself going back to school, starting a business, or working in a career that makes you feel fulfilled?

Do you want financial stability, emotional healing, or a strong, loving relationship? Get specific. Instead of saying, "I want to be successful," define what success looks like for you. Maybe it means earning a degree, launching a side hustle, or creating a stable home for your child.

Set Goals That Align With Your Vision

A dream without a plan is just a wish. If you want to change your life, you need goals that are clear and actionable. Think about what you want to achieve and break it down into steps.

If your goal is to finish school, it's not enough to simply say, "I want to graduate." Instead, you need a structured, step-by-step approach to make it materialize.

Start by researching schools or online programs that fit your schedule. As a young mom, flexibility is key, so look for institutions that offer part-time, evening, or online classes. Choosing the right school ensures that your education aligns with your daily life, reducing stress and increasing your chances of success.

Next, explore financial aid options. Many organizations offer grants and scholarships specifically for young mothers who want to further their education. Applying for financial assistance early can help cover tuition, books, and other expenses.

Creating a study routine that works around your baby's schedule is another essential step. Identify the best times in your day to dedicate to studying—whether it's during nap times, early mornings, or late evenings.

Finally, set clear academic goals for each semester. Instead of overwhelming yourself with a full course load, determine how many courses you can realistically complete while balancing motherhood. Having a structured plan helps you track your progress and stay motivated.

The same approach applies to financial goals. If you dream of starting a business, don't let a lack of money discourage you. Instead of focusing on what you don't have, shift your mindset to what you can do with the resources available. Today, there are more opportunities than ever to generate income online and build passive revenue streams, allowing you to create financial stability while maintaining flexibility. By embracing these opportunities and taking intentional steps, you can build a profitable business, create multiple income streams, and gain the financial freedom you deserve.

Shift Your Mindset and Overcome Limiting Beliefs

Attracting the life you want isn't just about external changes—it starts with your mindset. A lot of teen moms carry the weight of shame, self-doubt, and the belief that their dreams ended the moment they became a mother. Society often reinforces these fears, making young mothers feel like they are destined for struggle. But no matter what anyone has told you, your future is not ruined—it's still being written.

Your thoughts shape your reality. If you constantly tell yourself, "I'll never have the life I want," you'll find reasons to stay stuck. But when you start shifting your mindset and replacing limiting beliefs with empowering ones, you begin attracting a different reality. Instead of thinking, "I can't go back to school because I have a child," tell yourself, "I am capable of balancing motherhood and education, and I will find a way.

Take Consistent Action, Even in Small Ways

The life you want won't appear overnight, but every small step you take brings you closer to it. The key is to take action—

consistently and intentionally. Even if progress feels slow, every effort adds up over time.

Imagine a single mom who dreams of becoming a teacher. If she waits for the "perfect time" to start, she might stay in the same position for years. But if she takes small steps—researching certification programs, enrolling in one class at a time, or seeking mentorship—she sets herself in motion. With every step, she attracts the life she envisions, not by waiting but by actively creating it.

Life with a child can be busy and unpredictable; however, even with a busy schedule, you can find time to work on your goals. Wake up an hour earlier to study, use nap times to research opportunities, or swap social media scrolling for something that moves you forward. The more you align your actions with your goals, the faster you'll see progress.

Motivation fades, but discipline will carry you through when life gets tough. There will be days when you're exhausted from caring for your child, dealing with financial stress, or feeling discouraged. In these times, you have to remember success comes from showing up even when you don't feel like it.

Attracting the life you want isn't about making massive changes overnight; it's about being consistent in the little things that lead to big transformation.

Visualize and Speak Life Over Your Future

Your words and thoughts have power. If you constantly say, "I'll always struggle" or "I'll never have the life I want," that belief will shape your reality. But when you start speaking life over your future—affirming your strength, resilience, and ability to create change—you begin attracting different outcomes.

Picture yourself walking across the graduation stage, running a successful business, or buying a home for you and your child. See it so clearly that it becomes real in your mind. Most successful people, including young moms who have overcome adversity, started their journey by visualizing what they wanted and speaking it into existence.

The Right Environment and People

The people we surround ourselves with play a pivotal role in shaping our mindset, influencing our decisions, and ultimately impacting our self-worth. It's crucial to be intentional about the company we keep, as our environment can either uplift us or hold us back. I experienced this lesson firsthand when I lost the chance to obtain a certificate in geriatric nursing. People with mediocre mindsets surrounded me at the time. Their focus was not on achievement or growth, but on living for the moment and having fun. Their lack of ambition and responsibility gradually influenced me, leading me to adopt their unproductive habits. As a result, I lost sight of my goals, and the chance to become a nurse slipped through my fingers.

This experience taught me a valuable lesson: the importance of surrounding myself with people who inspire growth, ambition, and purpose. The right people are those who uplift us, challenge us to be better, and support our journey, even when we doubt ourselves. It's not about having a large circle; rather, it's about cultivating relationships that encourage and inspire.

Keep Pushing Forward

In life, especially as a mother, setbacks, disappointments, and unexpected detours are inevitable. There will be moments when things don't go as planned—when the path you envisioned seems far out of reach, or when the obstacles feel too overwhelming to overcome. It's during these times that it's crucial to trust and believe that God is guiding you, even if the road ahead isn't clear.

What might feel like a delay, a setback, or even a failure right now could be the very thing that sets you up for greater success in the future. Trust that God's plan for you is unfolding in ways you might not yet understand. The challenges you face today are building the strength, resilience, and character you need to achieve the life you desire tomorrow.

Keep moving forward in faith, knowing that everything is working together for your good.

Celebrate Your Progress and Inspire Others

Every small victory is proof that you are moving in the right direction. Whether it's finishing a course, securing a job, or simply making it through a tough week, celebrate your progress. The more you recognize how far you've come, the more confidence you'll have in where you're going.

And as you grow, don't be afraid to share your journey. There's another young mom out there who feels lost, just like you once did. When you rise, you show her that she can rise too.

Attracting the life you want isn't about waiting for the right circumstances—it's about creating the right mindset, taking intentional action, and refusing to settle. The moment you decide to move forward, everything begins to shift in your favor. Now, it's time to take that step.

Attract Who You Want To BE

To support you on this journey, I've created the Attract Who Want To Be workbook. It is designed to help you take action, stay focused, and bring your vision to life. Inside, you'll find exercises, reflections, and prompts that will empower you to make deliberate progress, track your growth, and stay aligned with the life you're working to create.

Alicia Whyle

PART 5
A LIFE RECLAIMED

CHAPTER ELEVEN

Lessons in the Rearview

As I write this chapter, my heart overflows with gratitude. Looking back on my journey, I see God's hand in every moment—every hardship, every lesson, and every victory. The pain, the embarrassment, and the anger that came with being a teenage mother never fully disappear immediately. They linger, resurfacing at unexpected times—a passing comment, a scene in a movie. For years, I found myself trapped in those memories, reliving them over and over.

It took me over a decade to finally break free from that cycle. My healing came when I rededicated my life to Jesus Christ, anchoring myself in His word. No longer do I carry guilt for having my son at sixteen. Through Him, I walk in righteousness—not by my own strength, but by His grace.

Today, my son is 22 years old, and he is nothing short of a blessing. Our bond is unshakable, and love is the foundation of our relationship. Though I would never encourage teenage motherhood, I can say with certainty that my son is one of the greatest gifts of my life.

Life often teaches us through the challenges we face, shaping us into stronger, wiser versions of ourselves. My journey as a teenage mom has been filled with hard-earned lessons, moments of growth, and revelations that changed not just my path but my entire outlook on life.

Here, I share some of the most valuable lessons I have learned.

Alicia Whyle

Mentorship is Key

One of the most profound lessons I've learned is the undeniable power of mentorship. Being a teen mom can lead to feelings of doubt, which can easily cause one to lose sight of their dreams and potential. Being mentored during this time is invaluable. A mentor offers guidance, wisdom, and encouragement, helping you navigate the challenges of life while also empowering you to build a better future. With the right mentor, you gain not only practical advice but also the confidence to make decisions that align with your goals and aspirations. Your journey doesn't have to be walked alone.

In the early stages of my life, I didn't fully understand the power of mentorship, so I turned to role models like Tony Charles—a character from Girlfriends. She was everything I aspired to be: confident, poised, and successful. But as much as I admired her, I eventually realized that life isn't scripted, and I needed a mentor who was real—someone who lived the values I wanted to adopt, someone who had actually walked the path I dreamed of walking.

I first came across Prophet Uebert Angel on YouTube at that time. I decided he was the person I wanted to follow. He became more than just a mentor—he became my spiritual father, a guide, and a successful businessman who embodied both spiritual wisdom and financial prosperity. His teachings illuminated my path in ways no preacher ever did. Prophet Uebert Angel's ability to break down the Word of God while aligning it with practical principles of success and prosperity spoke to me deeply. He was also a multimillionaire entrepreneur, embodying the very success I aspired to attract into my life. Through his teachings, I learned that success is not just about finances; it's about mindset, discipline, and faith.

Learn to Build Resilience

Life has a way of testing you, especially when you least expect it. For me, it often felt like every step forward was met with a storm determined to push me back.

I remember the moment I got accepted into university—a dream I had worked so hard for. But excitement quickly turned to dread when I saw the tuition fees. They weren't just expensive; they seemed impossible to meet.

I couldn't afford the first payment. Doubt began to creep in, whispering, "Maybe university isn't for you." Perhaps success was not in your destiny.

But something inside me refused to accept that. Determined, I organized barbecue fundraisers, waking up early to marinate meat, standing over a hot grill in the sun, and calling friends and family, hoping people would support. The smell of smoke clung to my clothes, and exhaustion weighed heavy on my body, but I kept going.

After weeks of effort, I counted the money I had raised. The amount I had raised was insufficient to meet my needs. The fear I had pushed aside came rushing back. The deadline was getting closer, and I had no idea how I would make up the difference.

Still, I refused to stop searching. I prayed, I hoped, and I held onto the belief that something—anything—would shift.

Then, just when I was beginning to feel hopeless, the unexpected happened. A cousin I barely knew reached out and offered to cover the remaining balance of my tuition. I was stunned and grateful beyond words.

That experience cemented a powerful truth in my heart: resilience, combined with faith, opens doors in ways you never expect. Even when the path seems impossible, when the odds feel insurmountable, the act of pushing forward is what makes the breakthrough possible.

Speak the Right Things

After having my children, I found myself struggling with self-doubt and negative thoughts that told me I wasn't good or beautiful enough. I carried these heavy beliefs with me every day, accepting the lies that kept me stuck in a cycle of insecurity. It felt like I was constantly battling against my own mind, unable to see past the pain and insecurity of my circumstances.

But everything began to change when my friend, who is now my husband, taught me a powerful lesson: "Your words create your reality." It was simple yet profound. Even when my heart was still filled with doubt and pain, he taught me the value of speaking highly of myself.

While this was a revelation, it wasn't until I encountered Prophet Uebert Angel's teachings that I truly understood the depth of speaking right. He spoke often about the power of words, emphasizing how they shape our future and angels are there to respond to our words. He explained that our words never die, and they have the power to either break us or build us up. The more I listened, the more I realized I needed to guard the words I spoke over my life. It wasn't just about positive thinking; it was about speaking with intention and allowing my words to shape my destiny.

Trusting Him

There were moments in my life when everything and everyone appeared to be failing me. The world seemed to be falling apart, and I was left to navigate the rubble alone. I didn't believe in myself. The weight of my struggles left me questioning my worth, wondering if I would ever find my way. But through it all, God remained faithful—though I often didn't see it at the time.

I've seen God's faithfulness in my life in ways I could never have imagined, especially in moments when it felt like nothing was working in my favor. One such time was while studying for my diploma. I was determined to do well, and I studied relentlessly for one particular module, pouring hours into reading. But when the day of the exam arrived, nothing I had studied came on the paper. I sat there, staring at the paper, feeling completely defeated.

At that moment, I did what I knew would work: I turned to God. I walked into the washroom and prayed. I poured out my heart to Him, asking for His help, knowing I couldn't do it on my own.

I returned to my seat, and something incredible happened—the Holy Spirit began to guide me. The answers began to emerge, and I confidently filled in the gaps one by one.

When the results were announced, I discovered that I had achieved distinction in the subject. It was nothing short of a miracle. In that moment, I truly understood the depth of God's love for me.

Looking back, I see how much God has guided me through difficult situations, and I know I would not be where I am today without His faithfulness.

The Value of Support

Walking a path like mine, from heartbreak and hardship to healing and victory, isn't a journey you take alone. You need at least one person—a steady pillar in the storm—who believes in your success even when you don't believe in yourself.

When I couldn't afford daycare to leave my boys and go to school, my friend stepped in. He watched them without hesitation, giving me the freedom to pursue my education. No one else offered that kind of help. Without his assistance, I would have missed numerous classes and could have put my dreams on hold indefinitely.

Support must come from someone you trust—someone who truly wants to see you rise. That person should possess the bravery to guide you back when you stray from your path and encourage you to keep going when you feel like giving up.

I'll be honest—there was a time when I got hooked on binge-watching Girlfriends. I would sit for hours, consumed by the drama, as entire days slipped away.

But my friend wasn't one to watch me drown in distractions. When he found out what was happening, he called me out on it without sugarcoating his words. Those DVDs, they went straight to the trash. It wasn't about denying me fun but freeing me from the kind of 'fun' that was quietly derailing my purpose.

That's what real support looks like—not someone who sits quietly while you sabotage your future, but someone who loves you enough to shake you awake when you need it most.

Balancing Responsibilities

Juggling the roles of a mother, student, wife, and business owner has been one of the most challenging yet rewarding experiences of my life. Finding balance required intentional planning, unwavering discipline, and a willingness to adapt when things didn't go as planned. It wasn't easy, but over time, I discovered strategies that made it possible to manage these responsibilities while still creating moments of connection and joy with my family.

One of the things I learned was the importance of setting dedicated time for each task. I carved out specific hours for schoolwork, business operations, and family time. I learned to distinguish between urgent and important tasks, which helped me focus on what truly mattered instead of being distracted by less critical demands. This structure enabled me to maintain my focus on essential tasks, preventing me from feeling overwhelmed by everything at once.

When it came to my children, establishing a routine was key. Homework was always a priority—completed after meals and baths before any other activities. Creating a consistent rhythm helped my kids know what to expect, making our evenings smoother.

Personal Development

Growth is a daily choice. Once I discovered the power of personal development, I committed to setting aside at least one hour each day for learning and self-improvement. Whether it's listening to preachers and motivational speakers on YouTube or reading a book, this habit keeps me motivated, renews my mindset, and helps me stay focused on achieving my goals.

Over time, this practice has strengthened my resilience and mental discipline. By dedicating time daily to motivational content and spiritual teachings, I continue to grow and push past limitations.

Personal Growth and Self-Acceptance

There was a time when being a young mother of three boys at just twenty years old felt like a badge of shame. Due to this, for years, the constant worry about what others thought of me had a powerful impact on my life. I let their judgments dictate my actions, my confidence, and my voice.

Years ago, I began writing this book, pouring every ounce of pain, victory, and truth onto the pages. But fear and shame stood as towering walls in my path. What would people think of me? Would they judge me? Would they see me differently? These questions echoed in my mind, even though people who heard my story were fascinated—amazed by the journey I had taken. Despite their encouragement, I couldn't shake the voices of doubt in my head. That fear kept me bound, silencing the words I longed to share.

Years ago, I chose to accept my past life, learn from my experiences, and use them as motivation to push forward and attract the life I desire. I no longer listen to what people say about me; my focus is now on what God's word says about me.

These lessons I've shared are not just reflections of my journey but guiding principles that have shaped my life. Embracing mentorship, building resilience, and speaking life into my circumstances have transformed my outlook and empowered me to attract the future I desire. By trusting in God's faithfulness and the support of those who believe in me, I've learned that every challenge holds potential for growth, and every setback is an opportunity for a comeback.

Alicia Whyle

The Strength in My Story

By the time I was twenty, I had already lived a lifetime's worth of experiences, pain, facing life's toughest challenges, and maturing faster than most. While my peers spent their youth chasing fleeting pleasures—parties, distractions, and temporary thrills—I was focused on survival. I worked, studied, raised children, and built a future from scratch. When I reflect on my journey, I see a stark contrast between my life and that of many of my old friends. They followed a predictable, comfortable path—secure jobs, routine lives, and little risk. I had no such luxury. For me, every step forward required intriguing choices, sacrifice, and a deep belief in the future I was determined to create.

Those choices were not without cost, but they ultimately propelled me toward a life of fulfillment that once seemed unattainable. I embraced challenges that others shied away from, pushing beyond limitations rather than accepting them as my reality.

Would I have taken a different path if I hadn't become a mother at sixteen? Perhaps. But one thing is certain—my son gave me purpose. He became the reason I rose above my circumstances and strived for a life greater than the one I had known.

Attract Who You Want To BE

Today, I stand as a woman before you, living a life I once thought was impossible. I have built a life filled with meaning, purpose, and success. But more than that, I've become a light for others—proving that no situation is beyond redemption, no struggle is wasted, and no dream is too far to reach.

This book serves as a testament to the strength that can emerge from the most challenging circumstances. My hope is that as you read my story, you find the inspiration to keep moving forward on your own journey. Personal resilience and the future you create shape your story, not your circumstances.

CHAPTER TWELVE

Two Roads, One Choice

In this chapter you'll meet young women whose unexpected motherhood forever changed their lives. Some chose to take action, fighting for their dreams, building futures they could be proud of. Others, paralyzed by fear, doubt, or the lack of support, struggled to find their way.

Their stories are real, raw, and full of lessons. These women show that your path is your choice, not your starting point.

Samantha's Story

I still remember the moment my entire world changed. I was sitting on the edge of my bed, gripping a pregnancy test in my trembling hands. I was only sixteen.

The experience of telling my mom was more difficult than I had anticipated. Her face fell, disappointment settling in her eyes. My dad barely spoke to me after that. The silence between us stretched for weeks, then months. Friends who used to text me every day suddenly had nothing to say. At school, teachers whispered when I walked past. I felt their judgment everywhere I went.

The only person who promised to stand by me was Marcus, my baby's father. He held my hand that first night and swore we'd figure it out together. But as the weeks passed, his messages slowed. The phone calls stopped. Then one night, he finally said he could not do this, and suddenly, he vanished.

The first few months were unbearable. Morning sickness hit me hard, making school feel like torture. I was exhausted all the time, barely making it through classes. I felt like dropping out many times, but I refused to let everyone be right about me.

I would lie in bed at night, staring at the ceiling, questioning how I could do this alone. There were times when I wished this pregnancy would end.

But then, on a rainy afternoon, my son, James, was born. And when I held him for the first time, I fell in love with hm. I had lost so much—friends, freedom, the future I once dreamed of. But in my arms, I held something even greater. This gave me a compelling reason to fight.

The next few years were a blur of exhaustion. The years were characterized by late-night feedings, early-morning classes, and part-time work at a shoe outlet to meet financial obligations. Some nights, I'd collapse into bed, tears slipping down my face, wondering if I'd ever make it in this world. But then, I'd look at Elijah, and I'd remind myself: I'm doing this for him.

At eighteen, I walked across the stage at my high school graduation with Elijah asleep in my arms. This diploma wasn't just proof that I finished school. It demonstrated my unwavering perseverance despite the world's disdain. Still, I wanted more.

So I enrolled in community college. The routine became second nature—classes during the day, work at night, motherhood 24/7.

I studied at 1 a.m. while Elijah slept beside me. Some nights, I got three hours of sleep, and some I didn't get any sleep at all.

At twenty-two, I earned my degree in business. But life didn't get easier just because I had a piece of paper. When I landed my first job at a marketing firm, I felt a sense of alienation. My colleagues had degrees from well-recognized institutions like Wales, while I only had my community college degree. I felt behind. But there was one thing I knew—I was not going to let that stop me.

So I outworked them. I learned faster and pushed harder. I had been fighting for my future since the moment I saw those two pink lines—I wasn't about to stop now.

By thirty, I stood in my own office, overlooking the city skyline. I had bought a home and sent Elijah to the best schools. I have built a life that I once thought was impossible.

Vanessa's Story

I still remember the night at my seventeenth birthday party when Sean and I decided to take a stroll on the cold beach. The moonlight was shining, and the stars were twinkling bright. That night we had sex for the first time right there on the sand. It wasn't until six weeks later that I began to experience nausea. I rush to the pharmacy to purchase a pregnancy test. I was afraid my mom saw the test, so I went by my friend Keisha to do the test. That night my life changed forever as I sat on the stairway at my friend's home. I was sitting there holding the test. A test I had prayed would be negative, but deep down, I already knew the truth.

I was a senior in high school. I had dreams—big ones. I wanted to become a nurse, to build a life beyond the tiny apartment my mom and I shared. However, those aspirations suddenly seemed to be slipping away from me.

When I told my mom, her face crumpled. She sat down slowly, rubbing her temples. She wasn't angry. She didn't yell. She just looked... defeated. I told her I was sorry, and I would figure it out. But deep down, I wasn't sure if that was true.

Lisa, a girl from school, was going through the same thing; she was three months pregnant. I will see her on her porch every morning, and I would ask, "You're not going to school today?" and she would reply, Those days are over for me until my baby comes. I can't bear the shame of people in school seeing me like this. It's just too much for me, she said. I told her she does not have to do it all at once; she can go to school online, but nothing I said could have changed her mind that was already made up.

Meanwhile, I pushed through my morning sickness, dragging myself to school no matter how awful I felt. The girls were mean, calling me names and looking at me with disgust, but I still push myself to school every day. I stayed up late studying, even when exhaustion made my body ache.

I worked a night shift at the street food outlet, saving every penny to prepare for my baby's arrival. I envied Lisa some days. While I was up all night working and finishing assignments, she was resting. But when I looked at my growing belly, I reminded myself—I wasn't just doing this for me anymore.

Then Ava was born. And suddenly, I understood sacrifice in a way I never had before. I went to class early in the morning with barely two hours of sleep, and I worked late shifts. Sometimes when I reach home, my baby is already sleeping. I remember being so busy trying to balance it all that I missed her first step.

The day arrived when I finally graduated with my high school diploma. Tears blurred my vision as I held my diploma. I had done it. Even though it was a joyful day, I felt a bit sad that Lisa wasn't there.

After graduation, I enroll at an online nursing school and eventually graduate with a nursing diploma. I worked at a private medical institute for some time, which paid enough for me and my little girl to live a comfortable life.

I hadn't spoken to Lisa recently because she left our neighborhood with her mom. However, a few years after graduation, I ran into her at a grocery store. Her once-bright eyes were dull, her face tired. She was bagging groceries. When she looked up and saw me, she was shocked.

We made small talk, but I could feel the weight of depression and stress in her words—the regret of not finishing school. As I walked away, my heart ached not because I felt sorry for her, but because I knew she could have been here with me.

We had faced the same storm that changed both our lives. The difference was I had chosen to fight through it. And that fight had made all the difference.

Mia's Story

I had planned to attend a degree program at Harvard University. My grades were exceptional, I was constantly thinking about my college dreams, and the future I had planned was coming together perfectly. However, everything abruptly fell apart.

Attract Who You Want To BE

I had always been careful. Always. But there I was at fifteen, staring at the positive pregnancy test in my hands, scared and in doubt. I had no answers. I couldn't decide what action to take next. Panic spun through my thoughts.

When I told my parents, the disappointment was immediate. I'll never forget my mother's face, the way her eyes hardened. Surprisingly, my father did not freak out as I thought he would, and I soon discovered why. That night, everything in my world crumbled.

I tried to hold it together, but the weight of my situation was crushing. I couldn't go back to my childhood room, no matter how much I wanted to. They told me I had to leave and figure it out on my own. My parents' fear of others' opinions led them to make such a harsh judgment.

I had nowhere to go. I wandered the streets, calling friends, only to hear the sympathy in their voices as they gently said they could not help me.

There was a shelter for teen moms someone told me about, and luckily it was only a bus ticket away. It felt like something was finally working in my favor. I walked in with my bag, and I met a woman named Ms. Rachel. She had been in my shoes, but she had made it through. She didn't pity me. Instead, she pushed me.

Ms. Rachel would assure me that I am not a hopeless case. "You're a survivor, Mia. That baby inside you is a reason to keep going, she said."

And so, I fought. I continued school online, and when my baby was two years old, I graduated from high school with the support of other moms in the group.

By 18, I received a scholarship for college. It wasn't Harvard, but the weight of what I had accomplished was surprising.

At 25, I had my degree and opened a daycare for teen moms, just like me. I knew what it felt like to be unsupported—to be left in the dark. I wanted to give other young mothers the chance I never had—the chance to dream beyond their circumstances.

Jordan's Story

My name is Alisha, and I am telling the story of one of my schoolmates, Jordan. She was a girl from my high school—another teen mom. I saw her every day in school; she was a top cheerleader. At seventeen she got pregnant by her teenage sweetheart Derrick. She was smart, passionate, and full of potential. But her story took a different turn.

She stayed with Derrick, the father of her child, a guy who made empty promises to change. He hurt her—physically and emotionally—but she stayed.

I tried to warn her. I told her, "Jordan, you deserve better than this. You can't let him treat you like this." But she believed in him more than she believed in herself.

I watched her drop out of school, let go of her dreams, and rely on him. Derrick kept promising he'd do better, but every promise was just another lie.

I lost touch with Jordan over the years, but when I saw her again when she was 26, I hardly recognized her. She was pregnant again for the third time. The toddler at her side looked at her with wide, unsure eyes. "You're still with Derrick?" I asked softly. She nodded, her eyes tired, the weight of regret hanging heavy in her gaze.

"I never thought it would be like this," she whispered. "I thought he'd change." She hadn't left. She did not go back to school, and now the cycle was repeating itself.

No matter how much I tried to help her, she kept saying it wouldn't work. Jordan did not believe in herself.

Alicia Whyle

The cycle had taken hold of her. She was another teen mom statistic, and I realized, with painful clarity, that some people have to break it themselves.

Akeila's Story

I was sixteen when I found out I was pregnant. At first, I thought the test had to be wrong. There is no way I could have been expecting a baby, I thought to myself. I was barely surviving as it was.

I had been living on the streets for months. My drug addict mother had kicked me out when I was fourteen, exhausted of dealing with a daughter she claimed had too much attitude. My father had never been in the picture. I had no one, and now I had a baby on the way.

I was scared and started having panic attacks. How would I feed a child when I could barely feed myself? How would I protect them when I had no home? Every day was a battle against hunger, exhaustion, and the weight of my own thoughts. I watched other girls my age laugh with their friends, go to school, and go to the mall wearing the best clothes, and here I am in a hopeless situation.

As my belly started to grow, I no longer wanted to be sleeping on the streets with other friends; instead, I decided to go and search for shelters so at least the life I am carrying inside of me can be safe. I came across a homeless shelter for domestic abuse women. Despite the absence of physical abuse, the lady running the shelter agreed to let me stay. It wasn't much—just a small room with a bed—but it was safe.

Ms. Karen, the owner of the shelter, took me to a website named Alisons.com, which offers tons of free courses. There I enroll myself in five business courses, learning about business ethics and computers. I committed myself to finishing those courses, and at the end I received five certificates.

On certain nights, I sobbed myself to sleep, filled with fear of failure. There were mornings when I felt like giving up. But every time my baby kicked, I reminded myself why I was fighting.

When my son, James, was born, everything changed. Holding him in my arms, I knew I would never let him feel the kind of loneliness I had felt. I worked harder than I ever thought possible.

I was able to land a business consultancy job because of these certificates, and by the time my son was three, we had a tiny apartment of our own. It wasn't much, but it was ours.

I know I could not have done it if I did not decide to come off the streets and the help of Ms. Karen. Looking back, I realize I was never truly alone. Strangers who showed kindness, shelters that gave me a bed, teachers who believed in me—all of it kept me going.

Emma Story

When I was sixteen, I got pregnant with my daughter Lily. My mom had remarried two years before, bringing a stepfather into our home who, behind closed doors, was nothing like the charming man everyone else saw. The sexual abuse started when I was fifteen years old. At first it looked innocent, like a kiss on the cheeks and then it escalated to me being raped numerous times when my mom was away. I was too scared and embarrassed to tell anyone.

I was terrified when I found out I was pregnant. Finding the courage to tell my mom was the hardest thing I'd ever done. She wavered between disbelief and devastation before finally believing me. What followed—the police investigation, court proceedings, and media attention—turned our small-town life into a public spectacle.

My mom eventually left her husband, and we moved to a new town, but that did not take away my pain or change my situation. My daughter, Lily, was born on a snowy February morning.

My mom helped support Lily until I could find something to do. Eventually I decided to go back to school online to get my GED. The pivotal moment occurred when I received an email from my English teacher, Ms. Rivera. She said I have incredible potential, and if I push a bit harder to increase my grades, I will be able to attend college.

Those simple words changed everything. Ms. Rivera connected me with a support group for young mothers and a community college program that offered childcare, which I enrolled in after finishing my GED.

College classes while parenting were brutal; I won't sugarcoat it. There were moments I nearly gave up—like when my laptop crashed the night before a major paper was due, or when Lily developed chronic ear infections and I had to miss classes.

Alicia Whyle

Surprisingly, I found unexpected strength in advocacy work. What began as participating in a support group evolved into me eventually leading workshops for other young mothers. I discovered my voice as a writer, publishing essays about resilience and trauma recovery that resonated with thousands online. I completed my bachelor's degree with honors, with Lily right by my side.

We cannot erase the past, but we strongly impact our future based on the choices we make. The nightmares still come sometimes, and there are days when the memories feel too heavy to carry. But I've transformed my pain into purpose, becoming an advocate for trauma survivors and now working toward becoming a counselor for at-risk youth.

A Heartfelt Letter For the Teen Mom

Alicia Whyle

A Letter For You

Dear Might Women of Valour,

I see you. I see the tears that fall silently on your pillow at night. I see how your hand instinctively rests on your growing belly, filled with both love and fear for the life within. I see how you walk with your head lowered, feeling the weight of judgment with each step. I've been exactly where you are, and I want you to know that you are not alone.

When everyone I trusted turned their backs on me, I felt a loneliness so profound it seemed to echo in my chest. The shame followed me everywhere—to school, to the store, even in my own home where the mirrors seemed to mock me with reflections of a future I hadn't planned. The sleepless nights weren't just from the baby's movements, but from the endless questions about tomorrow that kept my mind racing.

But here's what I learned, and what I need you to believe: the shame eventually quiets. Not because others stop judging, but because you begin to recognize your own strength.

The moment I decided that I wouldn't be defined solely as "the girl who got pregnant," everything shifted. Not overnight, but gradually, with purpose and determination. I reclaimed my right to dream again. I discovered that this unexpected path didn't close doors—it revealed new ones I hadn't considered before.

Your pregnancy is a chapter in your story, not the entire book. The decisions that brought you here don't have the power to write your final pages unless you hand them the pen. Take it back. Write boldly. Show the world—and yourself—what resilience truly looks like.

When you feel too weak to stand tall, lean on faith. There is strength beyond your own waiting to hold you up. With God, all things are possible—including the rebuilding of dreams you fear are shattered beyond repair.

Alicia Whyle

I challenge you today: lift your head. Walk as if you own the ground beneath your feet, because you do. Your worth isn't diminished by circumstance or by the opinions of those who haven't walked your journey. You have everything within you to achieve dreams even wilder than those you held before.

The broken pieces of your life aren't the end of your story— they're the foundation of something more beautiful than you can imagine right now. But this transformation begins with you believing it's possible.

I see your potential even when you can't. I believe in your future even when it seems distant and unclear. And I know with absolute certainty that the strength growing within you extends far beyond motherhood—it will carry you toward heights you never thought possible.

This is your moment.

Dream again. Rise Again. Reclaim your life.

From: A Sister Who Believes in You!

Attract Who You Want To BE

www.ingramcontent.com/pod-product-compliance
Lightning Source LLC
LaVergne TN
LVHW011942070526
838202LV00054B/4762